"Jerusha Clark exposes our secret thoughts, our strong appetite for approval, and the ineffective ways we try to patch up our faulty belief systems. With gripping honesty, she reveals the pitfalls that lead to despair and provides a map that guides the reader to embrace the One who loves her best."

— CAROL KENT, speaker and author of *When I Lay My Isaac Down* (NavPress)

"I love how Jerusha methodically exposes the lies we believe, rendering them powerless with biblical truths. Readers will learn to discover the freedom of knowing that they are wholly and completely loved by God, just as they are. Beautiful!"

— CONSTANCE RHODES, founder of FINDINGbalance.com and author of *Life Inside the "Thin" Cage: A Personal Look into the Hidden World of the Chronic Dieter*

"*Every Thought Captive* should be mandatory reading for every young woman. Authentic and immensely practical, Jerusha speaks from her heart and from God's Word. Don't read this book once; read it many times and be encouraged all over again."

— LORRAINE PINTUS, speaker and coauthor of *Intimate Issues*

"This is a must-read for all young women—and even some who aren't so young. Jerusha offers practical help and insightful wisdom to anyone struggling with self-acceptance and toxic thinking. I highly recommend this book to all my young-adult readers."

— MELODY CARLSON, author of the TRUECOLORS series and DIARY OF A TEENAGE GIRL series

D0071516

EVERY THOUGHT
Captive

battling the toxic beliefs that
separate us from the life we crave

JERUSHA CLARK

THINK

TH1NK
P.O. Box 35001
Colorado Springs, Colorado 80935

ISBN 1-57683-868-4

Cover design by Disciple Design
Cover photo by Veer; photo manipulation by Disciple Design
Author photo by Growing Family Portraits
Creative Team: Nicci Hubert, Kathy Mosier, Arvid Wallen, Bob Bubnis

Clark, Jerusha.
    Every thought captive : battling the toxic beliefs that separate us from the life we crave /
Jerusha Clark.
        p. cm.
Includes bibliographical references.
    ISBN 1-57683-868-4
    1. Thought and thinking--Religious aspects--Christianity. 2. Christian life. I. Title.
    BV4598.4.C53 2006
    248.8'6--dc22
                            2005031560

Printed in the United States of America

2 3 4 5 6 7 8 9 10 / 10 09 08 07 06

FOR A FREE CATALOG OF
NAVPRESS BOOKS & BIBLE STUDIES,
CALL 1-800-366-7788 (USA)
OR 1-800-839-4769 (CANADA)

To the women I love most . . .

my daughters,

Jocelyn Alexandra and Jasmine Alyssa,

in whom I see the women of grace and beauty God is fashioning

my sister,

Jessica Hoelle,

in whom I see fierce and loyal Love

and

my mother,

LeAnn Redford,

in whom I see Christ's victory through pain

Contents

EVERY THOUGHT CAPTIVE

FOREWORD

Dearest Reader,

Over the last decade I've come across many young women desperate to live their lives for Jesus yet slowed down on their journey by negative thought patterns. Despite their best efforts, these women just can't seem to break free. It's tragic to see women so full of potential and purpose enslaved by lies from the Enemy about who they are and who they can be in Christ. Thankfully I've also seen the other side: many, many women who in spite of deep-seated insecurity, difficult upbringings, or even abusive pasts have managed to overcome these toxic thoughts and find their way to freedom. And every time the antidote has been the same: truth.

I myself can testify to this. After being brought up on an emotional diet of verbal abuse and physical bullying, I soon started to feel the effects. By my teenage years I was totally off course, believing lies about myself and living out of them. But the grace of God found me, and the truth of Jesus set me free from this pattern. Years later I'm living, feeding, and depending on the very same truth every day. The truth of Jesus alone has the power to mend and to heal, to release and to restore, to encourage and to empower. Without it, we are thrown about in a stormy ocean full of deception and discouragement. With it, we stand with our feet on firm ground—the solid rock of Jesus Christ, the unchanging and unfailing One.

This is the powerful and inspiring theme running through *Every Thought Captive*. With helpful insights and honest testimony, Jerusha

Clark invites us to dwell on truth. She beckons us away from the perils of perfectionism, points out the dangers of living in insecurity, and highlights the paralyzing effect of fear on our spiritual walks. Along the way, she encourages us into a truth-inspired journey in which we dream and laugh and adventure with our God. But as Jerusha herself points out, this is no self-help book with a twelve-step formula guaranteed to bring you healing. Instead, her aim is to saturate you in the life-giving revelation of the Bible, the only power that can enable you to stop believing lies and move forward in truth. As she writes, "Though my words may fail you, God's Word will not."

The truth of Jesus transforms us. Let Jerusha and her wonderful words help you battle any toxic beliefs that keep you from the life you desire in God — and plug you into His wonderful and powerful truth.

Much love,

Beth Redman
author of *Soul Sister: The Truth About Being God's Girl* and coauthor of "Blessed Be Your Name" with husband Matt Redman

ACKNOWLEDGMENTS

Thank you to . . .

Kathy Hansen, whose friendship means more to me than a thousand words could express, who helps me live out the truth, and who gave me some killer suggestions during the writing process.

Kathy Moratto, who walks with me through the ravages and richness of life. Thank you for wrestling with me over the issues in this book.

Lorraine Pintus, who waged war on her knees for me and for this book. And who also read and dissected — with love and the Spirit's discernment — some of my early drafts.

Donya Duggleby, who counseled me in time of great need, whose spiritual insights challenge and heal me, and whose edits strengthened this book immeasurably.

Kristina Sklar, who edited tirelessly (during her pregnancy!) and who helped make this book life giving and hopeful.

Antonina Ruth, whose surgical editing savvy God used to deliver me in time of trouble. And who also is a riot and a sage.

Louie Moesta, mein K. S. and the most meticulous wordsmith I know, and Louise Moesta, who I admire and adore.

Nicci Hubert, who "got it" from the beginning, labored in love, and skillfully whittled the book into something passionate but palatable.

Heather Caliri, whose friendship and love help me find grace in brokenness.

Aunt Penny, who knows my heart inside out.

Janice Price, whose wisdom and pursuit of real life spur me on.

Katie Dorband, who compassionately ministers to me whether absent or present.

Cameron Germann, whose life compels me to persevere in prayer and to change the world.

Breanna McIntyre, who advances the kingdom with authentic and fiery love.

Kathy Orr, who is real and raw and right on.

Janice Rossen, whose online mentoring continually blesses me.

Kelly Fremon, who writes with passion and purpose.

Toni Fleischman, whose words of encouragement lift me up.

Nancy Sloan, Delores Thweatt, and Brenda Van Otterloo, who exhorted and celebrated with me.

Jen Matthis and Kelly Lainge, for sharing vulnerably on a January morning.

Kathy Walton, who, when I was paralyzed by pain, lowered me through the roof and into Jesus' presence.

Dr. Arlys McDonald, who asked me to go to the end of my thoughts and was willing to travel there with me.

Richelle Wissink, who inspired many of these ideas.

The ladies who work in the EFCC nursery, caring for my daughters with Christ's love: Jackie, Kristy, Kristen, Tomomi, Fumiko, Nancy, Janice, and Janette.

Everyone at Recovery Assistants Foundation, who believed and invested in me.

My prayer team, who volunteered to battle in the heavenly realms.

The courageous women who shared their stories for this book.

Kathy Mosier, who left no stone unturned.

My father, J. A. C. Redford, for reminding me what my name means.

Jeramy Alan, without whose love and support I could neither write nor experience the fullness of joy that I do.

And to my Lord Jesus Christ, who *is* the Truth, Love, Peace, Hope, and Life I crave.

CHAPTER 1

On My Mind

Thinking About What We Think About

In 2003, thanks to the groundbreaking work of Dr. Daniel Amen, I actually saw how my brain works. After a clinician injected my arm with small doses of radioactive chemicals, snapshots of my brain were taken using single-photon emission computed tomography (SPECT for short). Don't worry; you won't be tested on this.

The purpose of SPECT scans is to evaluate areas of a person's brain that work well, those that work too hard, and those that do not work hard enough. People who undergo SPECT imaging use this information to optimize their brain function.

Okay, apart from the radioactive injection thing (no, I don't glow in the dark), isn't that amazing? Wouldn't it be incredibly helpful to look at your brain and see which areas are right on target, which need some pep, and which need to take it down a notch? It was for me. And my SPECT-scan results made perfect sense.

Dr. Reed, the woman who reviewed my images, reported — very scientifically — that my brain was "on fire." She explained that parts of my brain, such as the basal ganglia and cingulate (which control anxiety and the ability to let go of obsessive, negative, or recurring thoughts and behavior) as well as the temporal lobes and deep limbic system (which she called the "inner critic" and "mood regulators"), were working overtime. Technically speaking, whether because of a chemical imbalance or my habit of dwelling on unhealthy thoughts (perhaps both simultaneously), my brain needed to settle down.

Do your thoughts ever seem overwhelming — uncontrollable, untamable, and completely ungodly, despite your best efforts to live righteously? Sometimes I'll review the thoughts I've had over the course of a day, even the course of an hour, and I'll despair: the mean things I've thought about others or myself, the impure, angry, or fearful thoughts that have assaulted me and reminded me how truly fallen I am. If these thoughts were displayed on my forehead for all to see, I'm sure I would live as a hermit.

You may be thinking, *Great, is my brain "on fire," too? What if I'll never be able to conquer the thoughts that pass through my mind? What if someone finds out what I'm really thinking about?*

There's nothing easy about asking yourself these questions, but you're in good company; every other woman on the face of the earth deals with the same thing. We all struggle with our thought lives, even if we don't know it. And talking with each other honestly about our thought lives rarely happens because it's vulnerable and uncomfortably close. Yet as I've matured, and as I've worked with other women, I've found that evaluating my thoughts, especially in the context of community, is *extraordinarily* important. What I think determines how I feel, which then impacts how I behave.

You may wonder what the big deal is. Perhaps you have no idea what's really going on in your mind because you haven't paid much attention. You think about whatever you want to think about and find it difficult to believe that your thoughts have much of an influence on your behavior, at least not directly. But consider Proverbs 4:23, which reads,

> *Be very careful about what you think.*
> *Your thoughts run your life.* (NCV)

Every act, whether beautiful or heinous, starts in the mind. Every charitable act begins with a loving thought, and every sin grows out of a distorted thought. We sin, in large part, because we hold on to and live out of toxic beliefs. So whether we are aware of the depths and brokeness of our thoughts or not, they are very real, and they influence us more than we even know.

Many of our thoughts, unfortunately, are both negative and untrue. At different points in their lives, most women have believed poisonous lies such as these: *I'm not good enough. What others think about me defines who I am. I am the sum of my accomplishments and my relationships.* We have believed a multitude of other self-defeating falsities as well, lies that have hijacked and poisoned our minds.

Getting to the Root

Joyce Meyer writes, "Thinking about what you're thinking about is very valuable because Satan usually deceives people into thinking that the source of their misery or trouble is something other than what it really is."[1] The Enemy wants us to believe that what we do is more important than what goes on inside us. But our behavior is only a symptom of a deeper problem.

Wouldn't it be wonderful if we could get to the real root of our problems? Judging from the fact that you decided to read this book, I'm guessing you're interested. First Peter 1:13,15 encourages us, "Roll up your sleeves, put your mind in gear . . . let yourselves be pulled into a way of life shaped by God's life, a life energetic and blazing with holiness" (MSG). A life and mind energetic and blazing with holiness — I think deep down that's what we all crave.

How and what we think determines our spiritual, emotional, and sometimes even physical health. Elizabeth George notes, "Like a virus, our thoughts have the ability to drain our energy and cripple our usefulness. Our thoughts can, however, also be a source of strength when we dwell on the powerful truths of Scripture."[2]

That's what we'll try to do together — dwell on the truth. I have written this book from a biblical viewpoint because the Bible both reveals Truth and defines how your mind was designed and is sustained by the living

God. You have been created incomparable and magnificently unique. No one thinks or feels precisely the way you do.

How Unique Are You?

Sadly, many people believe that to qualify as Christians, we must act, talk, and think in a similar manner. Truly, everyone should "learn to think like [Jesus]," as 1 Peter 4:1 teaches us to do (MSG). But we do ourselves a disservice by assuming that our minds, hearts, and souls can be shaped in a cookie-cutter fashion. Your faith does, and will always, look different from mine. You are *completely* unique. Forcing you to think or approach God like I do would be madness.

In their book *Prayer and Temperament*, Chester Michael and Marie Norrisey claim,

> One of the great tragedies during the past several centuries is that we have been more or less forced by training into a form of prayer or spirituality. . . . When it did not work, the conclusion was that there was something wrong with the person rather than with the method. The result was that many good people gave up . . . or went through the motions of [faith] without any real interior effect or benefit.[3]

One size does not fit all when it comes to spiritual formation.

With that in mind, I'll endeavor to steer clear of telling you exactly how or what to think in this book. I want you to understand and live in Truth as the woman *you* were created to be. I encourage you to filter each of the toxic beliefs and truths we'll discuss through the grid of who you are.

As you read, also keep in mind that I may not phrase the lies you've been tempted to believe in the exact words as those that poison your own thinking. Try, however, not to dismiss any of the toxic beliefs we'll explore simply because of phrasing. Instead, ask the Spirit if you've held to this misconception in any way.

My heart's desire is simply that you move toward a healthy thought life in order to become the person you were created to be. Which leads me to something important I'd like to explain about this book.

It's Not About Self-Improvement

I hope this won't disappoint you, but *Every Thought Captive* is neither a self-help book nor a guide for how to have a victorious thought life in 250 pages.

Rather, I want these words to lead you on a journey toward wholeness, inspired by the Lover of your soul. I pray that through this book, God will ignite in you a holy passion to evaluate and guard your thoughts. And I trust that the Word of Truth will act as an agent of renewal.

A pastor whom I deeply respect once said that the spiritual life is not about information but transformation. So it is with this book. I claim, for you and me, the words of the apostle Paul: "So here's what I want you to do, God helping you: Take your everyday, ordinary life . . . and place it before God as an offering. . . . Let God transform you into a new person by changing the way you think" (Romans 12:1, MSG; 12:2, NLT).

Your job? Just show up. Let Him have your troubled, full, exhausted mind. God will transform you into a new person by changing the way you think. Did you get that? *He* does the work. You give Him the room to do it.

Exposing my distorted thoughts to you and sharing the flawed mind-sets other women have confessed to me will be vulnerable and sometimes raw. Allowing the corners of your own mind to be illuminated may make you feel like a weak Christian or a bad person. Guilt often tells us that we've done too many bad things to change now. Shame says, "You are a bad person for thinking and acting the way you have [or are currently]." Please don't listen to these poisonous lies.

Enough Faith?

Before we dive into the many lies we believe, I'd like to debunk a particularly toxic belief, which tends to overshadow many others:

> *If I think or struggle with _____ [fill in the blank],*
> *I must not be a good enough Christian.*

The Enemy accuses and shames us with thoughts such as *How dare you call yourself a Christian? Look at your wicked thoughts!* and *If you had more faith, you would be over this struggle. You're so pitiful. What a failure! You'll never be as good a Christian as she is.*

Satan suggests ungodly things even to the most faithful, righteous women, and we cannot control him. He tempts all of us to believe lies that promise us freedom from pain, rejection, and lovelessness.

People also assault us with lies. We hear venomous messages every day about who we are and what we should be doing. Sometimes the world attacks us with such lies; other times (and how sad this is) Christians encourage us to live in deception.

There are even times when we choose to embrace distorted thinking. Often it's easier to believe that we're worthless and weak than it is to truly accept that in God we are incomparably valuable and girded with matchless strength.

Whether Satan, another human, or your own mind introduces a venomous lie to you, you have not failed even if an hour before — or after — reading about a particular toxic belief, you find yourself living out of it. You are not a terrible Christian; you are simply human. You are also not alone.

God knows that I am weak. He knows that I will fail. He knows your struggle, too. But your relationship with God is not based on how you perform. In success and failure, God sees you covered with the righteousness of Christ. He sees you as you will be eternally — perfected and purified. And God deeply desires your freedom from bondage; He never wants you to feel stuck in a life poisoned by lies. He wants you to be set free, and freedom comes by knowing and *living in* the Truth. We must vigilantly guard our minds, train them, and replace negative and misguided patterns of thinking with healthy and true ones.

I don't always discipline or protect my mind, and I'm willing to bet that you don't either. It's not easy. For much of my life, I actually preserved the purity of my mind pretty poorly. I've let thoughts run rampant and have struggled with a host of issues, all of which stemmed from unredeemed beliefs. Self- and body-image issues, bitterness, envy, depression, unhealthy relationships, and a variety of other problems wormed their way into my life through unguarded thoughts. I became a slave to my own distorted thinking. But Christ declared to me, and declares to you, "You will know the truth, and the truth will set you free" (John 8:32, NLT). In developing a relationship with Jesus, who *is* Truth, you and I experience the only true freedom.

James 4:8 also promises, "When you draw close to God, God will draw close to you" (TLB). What a mind-boggling thought. God, almighty God, will draw close to *you*. The fact that He wants me at all is sometimes difficult to grasp. But that He wants to be near to me? Intimate with me? That's breathtaking.

Throughout this book, we will draw near to God in the words we choose. You'll notice I sometimes miscapitalize words. This is to communicate that God is present in words that we often think of as things. Christ doesn't dole out love or hope as resources to be used up. He *inhabits* Love and Hope. He doesn't mete out mercy or grace. He *incarnates* Mercy and Grace. He doesn't define truth. He *is* Truth.[4] Love isn't merely a thing. It is the presence of God indwelling us, pouring Himself into and through us. Peace is not a thing that God gives, but a serene abiding *in Him*. We rest in assurance of things to come because He *is* Hope. We know grace because the Spirit of Grace dwells within us.

Through the following chapters, I will journey with you. Thoreau referred to books as friends with whom he dialogued. I hope you will see

Every Thought Captive—and me, too—as friends with whom you have a long, heart-to-heart conversation. We're in this together.

Why? Because I am not an expert on thought life. I have not completely conquered my thoughts—in *any* area. I still battle and need to be reminded daily of the very truths God has asked me to share with you. I simply seek to offer you biblical truths that God has taught me, the experiences of my life, and the stories of brave women who have shared their battles and victories with me. I pray that together—by God's grace—we might grab hold of the life we crave—a life marked by healthy, holy thoughts.

Many of us have heard that God commands us to "take every thought captive to obey Christ" (2 Corinthians 10:5, NRSV). But what in the world does that mean? By His grace, I propose we press into the mystery of taking every thought captive. Whether we recognize it or not, every woman's mind will be captivated by something. Some women live in bondage to poisonous misconceptions. They are captives to lies, myths, and deceptions. Other women live in freedom, captivated by Truth. You can see it in their eyes, hear it in the words they speak, and know it by the way they live and love. I want to be one of these women. I want to be a captive to real Life.

Through this book, in an effort to become women who truly live, we will expose and acknowledge the lies we have believed. Then, we'll allow truth to illuminate our minds and our paths. We will use the sword of the Spirit to combat the toxic beliefs that have held us hostage. We will embark on a quest for the captivated freedom Christ promises us. And we'll run toward—and grab hold of—the life we crave.

What Can I Do?

Throughout this book, I'm going to include specific thoughts about how Truth, rather than lies, can captivate our minds. At the end of each chapter, I will ask questions and give you ideas of what you can do to interact with the ideas we've explored. Use these in whatever way you desire, whether in personal meditation or group discussion. And over the course of our journey, I pray we will open our hearts and minds to God's radical transformation by doing the following:

- **Exploring His Word.** Each chapter in this book will expose toxic lies and uphold the truth of Scripture. Truth liberates us. Truth releases our thoughts from bondage to deception. Only Truth can transform us. Though my words may fail you, God's Word will not.

- **Identifying His voice.** I recognize some people's voices almost immediately. One word over the telephone, and I know it's my husband or my mom calling me. But it is not always so easy for me to distinguish the voice of God from my own or from the Enemy's. Contrasting lies and truths in each chapter will help us discern God's thoughts and identify His voice.

- **Applying Scripture to our situation.** It's sometimes easier for me to assent to spiritual truths as "wonderful ideas" than it is to believe that they actually apply to who I am and what I experience. But neither you nor I can allow the Word of God to remain abstract and impersonal. Knowing His truth doesn't guarantee transformation. Jesus asks us to practice what He's taught and exercise our faith. I hope the "On That Thought" section at the end of each chapter will help you and me authentically accept and *live in* Truth.

- **Confessing our failings.** The Enemy may redouble his efforts to hold you in bondage simply because you're starting to evaluate your thought life. Do not despair! We will all fail, but I encourage you: "When you catch yourself again, lose no time in self-recriminations, but breathe a silent prayer for forgiveness and begin again just where you are."[5] Many of us want to keep up the appearance that we've got things under control. We sometimes mistakenly believe that confession makes us weak. On the contrary, *our hidden defeats wear us down.* Confession brings incredible freedom; it takes power out of the toxic beliefs that poison our minds. Confession allows others to pray for us, help us see truth, and relate to us within their own struggles. As we confess to God and to others, we find our greatest strength — in Him.

- **Petitioning to the God who transforms.** James 4:8-10 commands, "Purify your inner life.... Get serious, really serious. Get down on your knees before the Master; it's the only way you'll get on your feet" (MSG). One of the primary channels God uses to transform us is prayer. Do you desire a purified inner life? Ask for it. Do you long to stand strong on your feet? Get down on your knees. Knock on the door of heaven and keep knocking until God answers with transforming power (see Luke 18:1-8 for a great example of persistent petitioning of God).

- **Going to the end of our thoughts.** I learned this practice from Dr. Arlys McDonald, and I am forever thankful. After I lamented to her one day about still getting zits at age twenty-eight, she asked, "So what does it mean if you have zits?" I thought out loud: "Well, then I won't be attractive." She countered, "And if you're not attractive, then what?" "Well, then people might not like me." "And then?" I was getting a bit frustrated at this point; I was also feeling *worse.* "Well, then I'll feel lonely and worthless," I blurted out. She smiled. (I didn't feel like smiling.) "Jerusha, *that's* the thought you have to fight." Arlys helped me see that when I think something like *I feel ugly* or *I feel fat*, there's a deeper self-doubt behind it. Sometimes what I really mean is *I feel unlovable and unacceptable* or *I feel weak and vulnerable.*

Have you ever felt this way? Many of us have never considered evaluating what's at the bottom of our thoughts. It's just too raw. Not to mention, it's far easier to say, "I feel _____ (fat/ugly/frustrated/worried/depressed)." But only at the end of — the roof of — each thought do we discover the toxic belief we need to confront first. As we do that, we find healing for the deepest of our doubts. More important, we find the Healer Himself. Will you draw near to God by going with Him to the farthest reaches of your mind?

~

Almighty God, who pourest out on all who desire it the spirit of grace and of supplication: Deliver us, when we draw near to thee, from coldness of heart and wanderings of mind, that with steadfast thoughts and kindled affections we may worship thee in spirit and in truth; through Jesus Christ our Lord. Amen.[6]

On That Thought . . .

1. Think about or discuss this quote by Frederick Buechner: "What deadens us most to God's presence in us, I think, is the inner dialogue that we are continuously engaged in with ourselves, the endless chatter of human thought. I suspect that there is nothing more crucial to true spiritual comfort . . . than being able from time to time to stop that chatter."[7]

2. Have you attempted to analyze your thought life before? If so, what did you find? If not, what gets you excited about this journey? What do you fear?

3. Journal about or discuss these statements: "Christ doesn't dole out love or hope as resources to be used up. He *inhabits* Love and Hope. He doesn't mete out mercy or grace. He *incarnates* Mercy and Grace. He doesn't define truth. He *is* Truth. Love isn't merely a thing. It is the presence of God indwelling us, pouring Himself into and through us. Peace is not a thing that God gives, but a serene abiding *in Him*. We rest in assurance of things to come because He *is* Hope. We know grace because the Spirit of Grace dwells within us."

4. What negative thought do you have about yourself or your life most often? Can you take that thought to its very end? What toxic belief do you find there? How might the Healer meet you there, at the far reaches of your mind? Ask Him to reveal Himself to you in this dark corner. Invite Him to transform (and keep on transforming) you there.

5. Have you ever thought, *If I think or struggle with* _____ [fill in the blank], *I must not be a good enough Christian*? How did you or could you overcome that thought with God's truth?

6. Do you believe your relationship with God is *never* based on performance? Do you live out that belief? Why or why not?

CHAPTER 2

GOOD ENOUGH

Recognizing Our True Worth

Each day it is absolutely crucial for me to listen for God's voice, affirming that I am God's beloved child. Only then can I resist the temptation to reinhabit my false identity. Only when I am listening to God's voice, and not my own, am I set free from having to prove to the world (or to myself) that I am worth loving, because God has already, repeatedly, affirmed his love for me.

FIL ANDERSON

I love my girlfriend Jaime's dramatic flair. When I first met her, she literally swept into the room wearing an electric green dress and matching tights. Jaime captivated my daughter Jasmine with the sparkly baubles on her necklace, but she fascinated me with her immediately transparent conversation and her intense, eyes-fixed-on-me listening. I adored her instantly.

Jaime and I found we enjoyed many of the same activities, liked the same kinds of exotic, extravagant foods, and read the same types of books. We also shared many of the same life struggles, chief among them the search for significance.[1]

The Chronicles of Jaime Winston

Ugly, unwanted, stupid, plain, boring, clumsy, unattractive, untalented, can't do anything right, useless, socially inept, too sensitive, too loud, too fat, too everything else, or too little of everything.

These thoughts formed a litany in my mind. And even when I could acknowledge them as lies, I couldn't stop myself from believing them. In many ways, these words became my self-definition.

I grew up in a solidly Christian home and went to a strong church. I heard that God loves me and thinks I am special. Teachers and family members told me I was talented and bright: "Jaime, you can succeed at anything you want to," they said.

During my tumultuous junior high years, however, I also became keenly aware of other people's, and my own, tendency to criticize and correct — sometimes harshly. Don't get me wrong: I knew they loved me and I knew God wanted me to accept myself, but even when I did something well or others tried to encourage me, I had a hard time believing their praise. I realized I wasn't all that my parents, teachers, or friends sometimes claimed I was, and I definitely saw the evidence of my many failings.

Looking back, I recognize that in my early teens, I surrendered to the self-defeating thoughts that other people, the Enemy, and even I introduced to my mind. Instead of asking God what He thought of me, I relied on my self-assessment and the opinions of others.

High school did not prove a time for bolstering my self-worth. Problems with friends concerned me. I hated my body. Lack of male attention grieved me (even though I didn't necessarily *want* to date the boys around me, it would have been nice for someone to fall madly in love with me). And self-deprecating thoughts increased daily.

I tried to improve my self-image with a list of accomplishments. I got good grades, won citizenship awards, ran the mile in under eight minutes. I was on the yearbook and newspaper staff, taught Sunday school, and even received a commendation from the state senate for my volunteer work. I thought, *I may dislike myself, but if I have this list of achievements, I will be all right.* The list would validate me and make me acceptable to the rest of the world. Or so I thought.

Through it all, I wrestled with God internally. I read His promises; I memorized some. I could spout off many of His Words of love and approval. Still, my heart and head lost connection. I believed His truth for other people; I could encourage them, but I could not believe that what He said applied to *me.*

I just never felt good enough for anyone — even God. I tried to stuff myself into the world's (and often the church's) round holes, but my square-peg self wouldn't concede. Eventually I stopped believing that I could change, that I could be who people wanted me to be.

It took a long time to acknowledge that the litany in my head was a pack of lies. They had become such a part of the fabric of my mind that I could barely differentiate between the toxic beliefs and reality, let alone God's truth.

But ultimately, I had to decide whom I would listen to. Would I let the torrent of self-deprecating ideas ravage my mind, or would I let His love stop the flow? Would I replay the tapes of critical judgment, or would I allow the tender words of Grace to invade my soul? God was saying, "Jaime, it's not too late; I make *all things* new!" "Jaime, I have loved you since before the earth's foundations were laid." "Jaime, I want you to be my friend and bride."

To live in freedom, to live in peace, I knew I must choose God. Only Mercy could help me yield false notions to the healing balm of Truth. Only Grace could equip me with the weapons I needed to wage war against the lies about who I am.

My quest for Christlike identity hasn't come to an end. It may never completely cease. But the Love that I have found, the Truth that has been revealed — even if in part — give me life and hope in the darkest of doubting moments.

Is This Your Story, Too?

My heart breaks with Jaime because I love her and because, in many ways, I share her story. I, too, have struggled with anxiety about who I am and what people think about me, with a sense of self-hatred, and with striving to validate myself through a list of accomplishments.

Like Jaime, I have asked, Who am I? What is my purpose? Do I matter? Am I lovable? Am I valuable? Am I living up to my potential? And, ultimately, who determines the answers to these questions?

Grace Himself met me in the depths of my questioning, for He is God of both skepticism and security. Unlike humans, God is not frightened by our struggles with identity. Instead, He beckons us to journey with Him through the deep-seated self-doubts and fears.

I urge you to come with me now to look at the deceptions that bind women like us to insecurity and self-doubt.

What Is God Thinking About You Right Now?

When I ask women what God thinks of them, I get responses like these:

- "God must think I'm a failure. I try, but I just keep sinning."

- "He has to be pretty mad at me. I know I'm not who He wants me to be."

Other women give me mixed messages:

- "God loves me. But He's probably angry at me right now. I've really been messing up."

- "God's love for me doesn't change, but He's probably upset that I'm not closer to Him."

Is this what God thinks about you, about me? Who is this God who loves us and died for us? What does He say about who we are? The way we answer these questions ultimately shapes what we believe about ourselves.

Therefore, let's discuss what kind of God we serve before we talk about anything else. If we harbor misconceptions about Him, we will never settle the deep, persistent questions about our identity.

What Are You Thinking About Him?

In Matthew 25, Jesus tells the parable of a master who entrusts his money to three servants before embarking on a journey. The first two servants invest what the master gave them; the third servant buries it in the ground. When the master returns from his travels, the first two servants return a profit on their master's investment. The third servant gives back what he'd been given with this explanation: "I knew that you are a hard man, harvesting where you have not sown and gathering where you have not scattered seed. So I was afraid and went out and hid your [money] in the ground" (verses 24-25).

Too often, like the third servant, we assume that God is harsh and demanding. We believe He'll be angry if we fail, so we'd better not try anything too risky. We don't believe we'll ever be good enough for Him.

From the first day I walked into church, I heard that Jesus loves me. I learned about His sacrifice on the cross: He loves me so much that He died to forgive my sins. I heard that He loves me too much to leave me the way I am, so He is going to change me and make me more like Him.

I believed a lot of that. But I also learned that I would never measure up (doesn't Romans 3:23 say we have all fallen short?), that I would one day be judged (see Hebrews 9:27), that on my own I can do nothing (see John 15:5).

As I took these verses and others out of context, I believed misrepresentations of the truth. But these distortions fit with what I assumed — that I wasn't good enough, that I would be found lacking, that I was always on the brink of failure, and that ultimately (if these other things proved true) nobody would love me.

To accept and embrace who we are, we must abandon our notion of a judgmental, exacting Master. Randy Rowland notes, "So many of us think God is standing around the corner . . . waiting to annihilate us for our most recent wrong."[2] Yet the Psalms assure us that our God

> *does not treat us as our sins deserve*
> *or repay us according to our iniquities.*
> *For as high as the heavens are above the earth,*
> *so great is his love for those who fear him. (103:10-11)*

Jesus loves us lavishly, showers us with delights, and treats us with mercy.[3]

This God, our Master, also knows well our sins, our failures, our weaknesses. He knows our faults before we confess them, before we commit even one offense. Yet He does not love us despite our sinfulness; He loves us — period. No becauses, no ifs, no whens. *No* conditions.

Author Madeleine L'Engle describes our sin as a solitary live coal, tossed into the sea of God's love.[4] His fathomless mercy triumphs over judgment (see James 2:13). *This* is the God we serve.

With this vision of God in mind, let's unravel some of the most prominent lies women believe about themselves.

What Are You Thinking About Yourself?

It's important to note that the myths we believe about self-worth, people pleasing, success, and control often determine what we do with our bodies, relationships, time, and money. And almost all of these lies influence our emotions — what makes us anxious or depressed and even what turns us on sexually. So in this chapter we won't cover *every* misconception about identity. Rather, we'll introduce some fundamentally false notions. That said, let's look at one of the most common distorted thoughts women believe.

LIE 1: *I'm not good enough.*

The first question I want to ask is this: Who do we need to be "good enough" for? How we answer this simple question will determine whether we will live in truth or bondage. If we reply, "For myself" or "For others," we will always come up short.

People often expect you to be different from who you are. They — or you — may never be entirely satisfied with who you are or how you perform. You may still feel the sting of past failure or the rejection of others. You may have battled self-hatred and condemnation for years.

And the Enemy, too crafty to stick with just one deception, which we might identify and challenge, may use different words (for example, *I'm unlovable, unacceptable, or unworthy*) to convince us that we're not measuring up. If he can keep us from feeling worthy, loved, and accepted, Satan knows that we will live in fear and insecurity.

We sometimes unwittingly aid him in this process, recycling painful judgments others made about us or self-abasing thoughts we've struggled with for a long time. The Enemy doesn't need to keep attacking us when we continually dwell on the negative, paralyzing thoughts that have poisoned our minds.

TRUTH 1: *I am more than good enough for Him. I am incomparably valuable, eternally cherished, and fully acceptable to Him.*

Please don't dismiss this truth as a spiritual platitude. God Himself is the one who declares your worth; every other opinion about your worth (even your own), while it may seem utterly important to you, is actually completely irrelevant to God.

I understand how it feels to care about other people's perceptions. I often care—a lot. But these fleeting, often false perceptions have no bearing on your true worth. God's view of you is the only one that really counts. And in God's opinion, you *are* good enough. He not only allows but *longs* for you to live in His holy, radiant presence for eternity (see Philippians 3:20). He is not ashamed to call you His own—His friend, His child, and His beloved (see John 15:15, Romans 8:14-17). And in Song of Solomon, He proclaims, "My darling, you are . . . beautiful" (6:4, NCV). You, my sister and friend, are good enough for God. This is not just true for me or for your friends, but for *you*.

Perhaps you've heard these things before. I had. I heard them and thought, *Oh, that is so wonderful. Okay, so I am good enough for God.* Then I promptly started trying again to prove my lovability and worth by performing for others. I may have known the truth, but I didn't allow it to affect my daily life. The people I performed for most were my friends, my boyfriends, my family. But even when I succeeded at garnering their favor, it lasted only so long. And worse, I rarely felt satisfied. I always felt as if I could do better, be better.

I think my dissatisfaction came because the sort of approval I received was neither eternal nor truly valuable. Only when I embrace God's true love for me will I find satisfaction with myself. As Thomas Merton says, "Whether you understand it or not, God loves you, is present in you, lives in you, dwells in you, calls you, saves you and offers you an understanding and compassion which are like *nothing* you have ever found in a book or heard in a sermon."[5] In Jeremiah 31:3, God declares, "I have loved you with an everlasting love." He cries, "Do not be afraid, for I have ransomed you. I have called you by name; you are mine. . . . You are precious to me. You are honored, and I love you" (Isaiah 43:1,4, NLT).

Catherine of Siena described God as *pazzo d'amore* and *ebro d'amore* ("crazed with love" and "drunk with love"). What an incomprehensible, beautiful image: God, the One and living God (the God many people see as a cosmic spoilsport!), intoxicated with love for us. For *you*.

Have you longed, as I have, to be loved in this way?

John Eagan took the following advice from his spiritual director: "The heart of [life] is this: to make the Lord and his immense love for you constitutive of your personal worth. Define yourself radically as one beloved by God. God's love for you and his choice of you constitute your worth. Accept that, and let it become the most important thing in your life."[6]

These are the truths — who God is and who we are — on which our entire faith is built. These truths are the core reality of our very existence. They can bring freedom like we've never known.

It took me a long time to acknowledge these most fundamental truths: I am good enough, worthy enough, lovable enough, and fully acceptable to God. And I am still learning to live in this reality.

LIE 2: *Failing means I am a failure.*

Do you ever avoid something because you're afraid that if you fail at it, you'll be judged or even mocked? Have you ever feared that failure makes you worthless?

Conversely, like Jaime and me, have you ever tried to prove your worth by listing your achievements? Did the list keep you from doubt and self-hatred? It didn't for me.

TRUTH 2: *Performance dictates nothing about my worth.*

Even though it's hard to accept, the truth is, your list of achievements has nothing to do with your worth. Some of us pretend to accept this truth because we know we should, but our acceptance is rarely authentic or lasting. Many of us continue to perform for approval or perceived success.

But God does not condition His love or your value on what you do — *ever*. He does not love you more if you are a "good" girl. In God's eyes, you are like the most brilliant diamond — the one displayed in a pristine glass case at Cartier, the one that can be sold only to the highest bidder. You are so valuable that "you were bought at a price" (1 Corinthians 6:20), the highest price one can pay — Life Himself. And He never stops loving you, not even in your worst moments: "The unfailing love of the LORD *never* ends!" (Lamentations 3:22, NLT, emphasis added).

The world tells us that success matters most. The world tells us that if we fail, we are nothing. God, on the other hand, tells us that any good we do, anything we accomplish, comes as a result of our already complete worth. He also tells us that even when we sin horribly, what we've done does not define our value.

When you said yes to God, He declared your eternal victory. But in the meantime, through life's cycle of ups and downs, achievements and flops, we often need to be reminded that our identity is never conditioned on our accomplishments. He promises to help you recall this truth; you need only listen and *believe.*

LIE 3: *If I perform well, I won't face failure or rejection.*

This is the lie that causes some of us to strive for the unattainable — perfection.

Brennan Manning writes, "It used to be that I never felt safe with myself unless I was performing flawlessly. My desire to be perfect had transcended my desire for God. . . . My jaded perception of personal failure and inadequacy led to a loss of self-esteem, triggering episodes of mild depression and heavy anxiety."[7]

I understand these words. As it did for Manning, perfectionism led me to deep despair and fear. Perfectionism promised me self-assurance but ultimately delivered self-doubt. Early in life, I discovered that if I could keep most people happy by working really hard at being a "good" girl (student, friend, daughter, girlfriend, wife, and so on), I felt better about myself. But I also discovered that my attempts to win approval based on being "perfect" bolstered my self-image only temporarily. As new challenges came my way, I would again wonder, *Will I cut it this time? Or will I ruin everything I've built up by failing now?* I also found that even if I did perform in a way that people perceived as perfect, it did not guarantee I would think positively about myself. Others may have praised me for being particularly kind or generous, but I knew that my motivation for doing acts of seeming magnanimity was sometimes not so noble.

Psychologist David Seamands claims, "Perfectionism is the most disturbing emotional problem among evangelical Christians. It walks into my office more often than any other single Christian hangup."[8] Wow. Like Dr. Seamands, I'm distressed by Christian perfectionism (by my *own* perfectionistic habits) because the Bible clearly teaches we have all fallen short and will continue to miss the mark. If we took God at His word, none of us would be playing the perfection game. But somehow, somewhere along the line, many of us decided that we should at least try to be perfect, to display no weakness. What a deadly lie.

TRUTH 3: *I cannot be perfect because I cannot be God.*

Deep down, we know we cannot be perfect. Even if others think we are, we know our own failures. Yet many of us keep trying, striving, reaching.

The seed of perfectionism resides within the oldest lie in the Book — "you will be like God" (Genesis 3:5). Ever since Eve ate the forbidden fruit, women have tried to "be like God" — controlling everything, measuring up to every standard, avoiding failure.

Some Christians try to rationalize a certain degree of perfectionism by quoting Jesus' words in Matthew 5:48: "Be perfect, therefore, as your heavenly Father is perfect." What Jesus asks us to do here is not strive for perfection but rather recognize that without Him, we cannot be holy, as the Father commands us to be. Only by accepting Christ's sacrifice do we become both eternally perfect in the Father's eyes and able to be sanctified, to be perfected into who we already are: joint heirs with Christ.

It took me quite some time to recognize that perfectionism is basically an effort to be God. But as I drew near to Him, God showed me that when I struggled to do everything perfectly, I also worked to bring glory to myself. I wanted the praise, the approval, the satisfaction. My performance and the accompanying benefits became an insidious idol.

Serving the god of self, the god of perfectionism, did not make me happy. We are most fulfilled when we do what we were created to do—bring glory, honor, and praise to God, not to ourselves. I have found the surrender of perfectionism a much more successful, liberating endeavor than the fight for it.

What relief it brings to let go of straining so hard. That is why Jesus says to us,

> "Are you tired? Worn out? Burned out . . . ? Come to me. Get away with me and you'll recover your life. I'll show you how to take a real rest. Walk with me and work with me—watch how I do it. Learn the unforced rhythms of grace. I won't lay anything heavy or ill-fitting on you. Keep company with me and you'll learn to live freely and lightly." (Matthew 11:28-30, MSG)

The unforced rhythms of grace—doesn't that sound good?

LIE 4: *People can't really change.*

Some women strive for perfection, but others, based on the belief that they can't change, simply resign.

Have you ever had thoughts like these? *I'd better just get used to who I am. I don't even know why I try. If I really fail, at least I'll be good at being a failure.*

I suppose I should not entirely separate these feelings from those of perfectionism. I know that I have personally vacillated between the driving thoughts of *Try, try, try* and the hopeless notion of *Just give up; you won't ever make it.*

Some of you grew up in homes where the predominant messages were, "You're good for nothing. You'll never amount to anything." Perfectionism is a joke to you; it's hard enough to try anything, let alone

36

do something perfectly. Even if these words were never verbalized, the idea that you could never change may have been communicated loudly enough.

My friend, I grieve with you. You've endured heartbreaking things. You've been told venomous lies. I pray that God would heal the ache of your heart and bind up your wounds. Jesus can help you go forth in new life; He can make all things new. God does not want you to live regretting the past and fearing the future. He can change everything—your perception of yourself, your circumstances, your bondage to a sinful lifestyle, or your frustration with seeming to be unable to grow and mature in Him.

TRUTH 4: *Because of Christ, I have been transformed and am, at this very moment, being transformed.*

When you first came to know Christ, you may have heard the verse, "Therefore, if anyone is in Christ, he is a new creation; the old has gone, the new has come!" (2 Corinthians 5:17).

Did you believe that? Do you believe it now? Do you believe that the old you has gone and that God made you new at the moment of your conversion?

The evidence of life seems to contradict that verse. We do not instantly appear new when we believe in the Lord Jesus. We still struggle with sin and shame. We still live in bondage in many ways. But Jesus promises that we are "being transformed into his likeness with ever-increasing glory, which comes from the Lord, who is the Spirit" (2 Corinthians 3:18).

We can't always tell that we are being transformed because our vision is not like God's. Unlimited by time, He can view us as we are and as we will be. His perception of us is not based on isolated moments, nor does He see us only against the backdrop of our past. Instead, God knows who we are *right now*—a new creation—and who we are *becoming*—the sanctified bride of His beloved Son.

We often lament because we still don't have victory over the same sin that beset us the day we repented. And our hearts stagger under the weight of past sin. Aren't we supposed to be free of this shame? Yes! We are free. Although you continue to stumble, as we all do, you have been liberated from both the wages and shame of sin.

At the Cross, Jesus took the entire weight of sin upon Himself. Christ's burden on Calvary included the guilt and the shame of every one of your transgressions.

You *are* free. And you *can* change, whether it's sin, shame, or pain that plagues you. Jesus already purchased your triumph and is actively working with you, right now, to release you from the bonds that try to hold you in a vicious "old you" cycle. You don't have to give up on or punish yourself.

First John 3:19-20 says that we can "be confident when we stand before the Lord, even if our hearts condemn us. For God is greater than our hearts, and he knows everything" (NLT). The first time I really read this verse, I was on a mission trip in Mexico, feeling guilty for falling into an old pattern of sin. It's hard to express the radical freedom I felt in understanding for the first time that God knows my heart and that I don't need to condemn myself.

Right now we cannot fully comprehend the mysterious glory of God's timeless vision. We cannot see how we can be all at once flawed yet perfect in His sight. But we *can* trust that He is good. We do not have to live in resignation. We don't have to avoid risks because we're afraid to fail.

Through the prophet Jeremiah, God promises, "I have good plans for you, not plans to hurt you. I will give you hope and a good future" (Jeremiah 29:11, NCV). Don't let these familiar words pass you by! God is not setting you up for failure, nor does he see you as a failure — ever. He has long planned for your future, and the plans He has made are good, hopeful, sure. As you lean on Him more each day, you will be able to see how He is transforming you.

LIE 5: *If I can stay in control (if I am strong), then I'll be safe.*
I like to be in control because it makes me feel safe. If things are out of control, I assume I must have done something wrong, which would make me unacceptable and vulnerable.

The lie that I could mask my self-image issues under a veneer of control sucked me under. I thought if I appeared—and if others perceived me as—unshakable and on top of things, I must be in control (or at the very least, no one could suspect me of having problems).

Some of you have been taught that only the strong survive. The weak are kicked around, brokenhearted, needy, helpless. You may have endured terrible verbal, physical, or sexual abuse and decided that you would never allow another person to wound you. You may have witnessed abuse being inflicted on someone you love. You may have heard from your culture that women should be in control of all things and that in order to get ahead in this world, women must not show weakness. Or you may just like the feeling of being in control.

This can quickly become your identity. You need no one, you keep at bay others who threaten your position in any way, and you get what you want when you want it—*or else*. If someone tries to help you, you forcefully communicate, "I don't need you or your advice. I am perfectly capable of handling life myself."

But the problem of human weakness always remains. You cannot stay strong perpetually. No one can. If you attempt to do so, your forceful exterior may hurt others in the same way you were once wounded.

People are uncontrollable. I see that every time my daughters get sick and I have to rearrange my whole day—my sleep, my activities, my attitude—around them. Many situations are uncontrollable. I see that every time I get in line at the post office and two of the employees simultaneously go on lunch break, leaving the *Guinness Book of World Records'* oldest postman on duty—alone. Even my emotions are often uncontrollable. I see that every time I burst out in unbidden rage or in tears, especially at those moments when I most want to control myself.

Sure, we can keep a few things (sometimes quite a few things) under control, but we cannot do so indefinitely. Many of us get knocked upside the head with an uncontrollable situation and *still* try everything in our power to bring it under our control, despite our failure to do so.

Truth 5: *True strength and safety come through surrender.*
In Psalm 62:6-8, David proclaims,

> *[God is] solid rock under my feet,*
> *breathing room for my soul,*
> *An impregnable castle:*
> *I'm set for life.*
>
> *My help and glory are in God*
> *—granite-strength and safe-harbor-God—*
> *So trust him absolutely, people;*
> *lay your lives on the line for him.*
> *God is a safe place to be.* (MSG)

God is a safe place to be; He is rock solid. In Him you are set for life. You can trust Him to control things.

The phrase *control freak* often applies to me. When I shared this with Nina, one of those rare, kindred-spirit friends, she confessed that the term also describes her sometimes. Almost in the same breath, she related to me the most amazing, intimate story of how God is starting to remind her of two things—she is not in control, and His sovereign provision is perfect:

> Nearly every afternoon when I check the time, it's exactly 4:21. I discovered while reading in Romans that verse 4:21 refers to Abraham's faith (and his wife, Sarah's, disbelief) that God could control things better than they could. When Sarah tried to manipulate circumstances, Ishmael, the son of enmity was born. When Sarah and Abraham surrendered control to God, however, the promised son, Isaac, whose line eventually led to Christ's birth, was brought into the world.

God's plan is always better than our own. His ways are always better than ours. He will remind us of it (perhaps at 4:21 every day) and will continue to invite us to surrender our efforts to keep things under tight wraps.

This is no easy task for those of us who have become accustomed to controlling situations and people to get our way and feel safe. I, for one, do not like to be weak. I hate feeling raw and vulnerable because I'm scared I will be found lacking.

But God has given me hope in this through one of the greatest paradoxes of the Christian life: "When I am weak, then I am strong." In 2 Corinthians 12:9, God proclaims that He is "with you; that is all you need. My power shows up best in weak people" (TLB). In response to this, we can boldly proclaim with the apostle Paul, "Now I am glad to boast about how weak I am; I am glad to be a living demonstration of Christ's power, instead of showing off my own power and abilities. . . . When I am weak, then I am strong — the less I have, the more I depend on him" (verses 9-10, TLB).

Releasing the reins of your life and acknowledging your weakness may seem risky, even downright terrifying, but the Lord promises that He is a safe place to be. He will not forsake you. If you have been hurt in the past, let me assure you that "He will not crush those who are weak or quench the smallest hope. He will bring full justice to all who have been wronged" (Isaiah 42:3, NLT).[9]

As we close this section, let me emphasize that reading these truths will not immediately accomplish the work God intends to do through them. We must differentiate between knowing the truth ("Yeah, yeah, yeah, God loves me and accepts me. *But . . .*") and truly living out our beliefs. Genuine transformation occurs only as we let Truth sink down into the very core of who we are, changing our thoughts and our behaviors.

Our minds are renewed through a process over time. You may wish to reread this section as you work through some of the forthcoming chapters. Authentically believing (living in) the truths about who God is and who you are enables you to confront the lies we'll discuss together in this book.

May God continue to woo you, His beloved, into a secure identity, grounded in Him.

What Can I Do?

- **Ask Him to remind you.** After reading this chapter, my girlfriend Kelly sent me an e-mail. She wrote, "Jerusha, I know this is true. But I could tell myself five hundred times a day that I am good enough for God and still not believe it." I asked her (and I ask you), "Have you ever tried?" Many of us are so busy going about our I-am-what-I-can-accomplish lives that we fail to commune with the God who is enticing us to Real Life. He wants us to live out the truth, but we can't do that without hearing from Him every day. When I am listening to Him daily, attentively, I find it easier to confront the toxic beliefs that tempt me into insecurity, self-condemnation, and controlling, perfectionistic, or resigned living. Start by asking Him to remind you who you are—even five hundred times a day.

- **Believe that what He says applies to you.** During this chapter, have you thought, *Well, that's nice, but "the Beloved"? That's not me—not yet, at least.* When I say, "You are God's friend, His daughter, His true love," do you believe that? I used to be a master of applying Scripture to encourage and uplift others, but I could just as craftily twist Scripture to lock myself out of God's love. I am learning, by His grace, to live in the reality that His Truth is mine. You can learn this, too.

- **Consider what you call yourself.** As we seek to develop a godly self-image, we must not merely assent to the truths of Scripture; we must keep our vocabulary in step with our beliefs. Whether we realize it or not, calling ourselves dumb, annoying, awkward, and so forth really impacts our self-perception. Do any thoughts like these stay trapped in your head? At one time, when I would do something wrong or bad, the words *stupid b*%@#* flew into my mind. At first, I recoiled at this nasty name. But after a while, these words became so much a part of the framework of my thinking that I could no longer fight against them. Finally, I confessed this to Donya. She listened compassionately. Then she told me gently, lovingly, honestly, "Jerusha, God would never call you that. It's a lie from the pit of hell, and you can rebuke it with the truth of God's Word." I needed someone to point out that what I was thinking was a *lie*. I had lost the ability to separate my feelings from the truth. Donya helped me do that. If you find negative names popping into your head, speak God's truth to yourself and ask others to help you refer to yourself by the true names God calls you: beloved, precious, radiant, beautiful, holy, treasured.

- **Recognize that you may confront these lies again and again.** David Seamands writes about our tendency to slide back into old thought patterns. He notes, "Part of [the] mind believes in God's love, accepts God's forgiveness, and feels at peace for a while. Then, all of a sudden, everything within . . . rises up to cry out, 'It's a lie. Don't believe it! . . . How could God possibly love you and forgive someone like you? You're too bad!'"[10] I have faced the same lies again and again. Often I have despaired: "Lord, am I not done with that one?" But over and over, His voice comforts me: "I am all that you need. My power shows up best when you are weak" (remember 2 Corinthians 12:9-10?). Try not to fret when the lies crop up — again. His truth withstands all tests, no matter how many times they come or how powerful they seem.

~

May today there be peace within. May you trust God that you are exactly where you are meant to be. May you not forget the infinite possibilities that are born of faith. . . . May you be content knowing you are a child of God. . . . Let this presence settle into your bones, and allow your soul the freedom to sing, dance, praise and love. It is there for each and every one of you.[11]

On That Thought . . .

1. Take five minutes to describe God. Don't edit yourself — be completely honest (don't worry; He's heard it all before).

2. Take five minutes to describe yourself. Same rules apply. Don't self-edit. Then reread what you've written here and in response to question one. Use a highlighter to mark any lies you have believed about God or yourself. If you are feeling especially brave, read what you've written to someone else.

3. Place all the words you wrote in front of you. Ask the Holy Spirit to still your mind and make you attentive to His voice alone. Set a timer for five minutes and sit silently before the Lord. Listen. What is Truth saying about Himself? About you?

4. What images do the words *beloved*, *precious*, and *radiant* conjure up in your mind? Why? How has the Enemy distorted these

words, keeping you from relishing the beautiful truths of who you are in Christ?

5. Which of the lies we've confronted in this chapter seem to trip you up most often? Go back in your mind to the first time you remember thinking those distorted ideas. Ask God to help you reach as far back as possible. Invite His redemptive grace to heal these memories.

CHAPTER 3

WORRIED

Knowing the Real Fear

Is anxiety a disease or an affliction? Perhaps it is something of both. Partly... because you can't help it, and partly because for some dark reason you choose not to help it, you torment yourself with detailed visions of the worst that can possibly happen.

FREDERICK BUECHNER

Have You Ever Felt Like Tina?

You never know when or where you'll meet an amazing person. I came into contact with Tina at the ice cream shop where she works. By my second or third visit to Scoops (anyone who knows me will testify that I am a frozen dessert–aholic), Tina and I found common ground for a friendship — passion for Christ and a desire to help others grow in Him. When I went in to feed the ice cream monster within me, Tina and I began asking each other get-to-know-you questions. The humility and authenticity with which she spoke drew me in and even inspired me.

I wanted to get to know Tina better, so we met at Starbucks one Monday morning. Over coffee and crumble cake, Tina and I discussed everything under the sun, including her struggle with anxiety. I asked if she would allow me to interview her for this book. She graciously let me into her private world for a moment, describing for me her physical/emotional/spiritual battle. She also offered to share her experience with you.

> Sometimes, overwhelmed by an underlying sense of worry — whether it's about what's happening at school and in my relationships or something more nebulous like "my future" — I wake up in the middle of the night, right in the worst moments of an anxiety attack. My heart races, my arms and hands feel tingly. My whole body seems light, faint, weak. I shake and sweat. I try to stand but swoon with dizziness. My face drains of color, and I can't catch my breath.
>
> When it first started happening, I tried really hard to dwell on the promises in God's Word. I reminded myself that Jesus will never leave or abandon me; on the contrary, the Lord assures that He will protect and care for me.
>
> I know without a shadow of a doubt that this is true, but I still have a hard time applying His words to the specific circumstances that come my way. Actually, it's difficult for me to even imagine living without fear, concern for my future, and regret over my past.
>
> Yet I definitely don't want to experience any more panic attacks. Sometimes I think it might be better to feel nothing — to be numb — than to be afraid all the time. When it comes down to it, I just don't want to feel pain. I don't want to know that I could have done better and didn't. I don't want to wonder forever what will happen if I let go.
>
> I want to trust God. I believe He's trustworthy, but . . .

How Much of Julia Is in You?

Julia once confessed to me that she worries all the time. I told her, "Welcome to the club." We had a good laugh at the old term *worrywart*, but Julia admitted that word pretty accurately describes her life.

Like a wart, worry is unwanted, uninvited, and even ugly. As we would with warts, we try to cover up our worry. We often stuff it underneath a scriptural Band-Aid. But in the quiet moments, Julia says, she picks at "what if" and "if only" warts over and over again.

Curious, I asked her what she worries about most. She seemed a little embarrassed.

Well, it's usually nothing major — you know, just day-to-day stuff. Did I turn the light in my closet off? Will they cancel our reservations if we're late? I just ate spinach salad — is there green stuff stuck between my teeth?

Sometimes I fret over bigger issues, though. For instance, I just found out that my company will be doing layoffs in three months. I try to leave it in God's hands, but *three months* of worry seems pretty daunting.

I also worry about my mom's deteriorating health. And I fear getting ill myself. With all of the scares these days, I have trouble not reading into aches and pains. But when I start giving in to a fearful thought, it sort of explodes in my mind.

You know what's funny — and frustrating? Most of what I fear doesn't happen. Even when something I've felt anxious about *does* come true, the pain that comes with it is almost never as bad as the constant, stomach-sick anticipation of "what might be."

At twenty-five, I've just started to learn that when God tells me to "be anxious for nothing," He means *nothing*. I've got to tell you: It's painstakingly hard for me, but I am starting to live out the trust I claim to have in God.

Do You See Yourself in Kara?

Kara is one of those bright lights in my life — fun, godly, always has an encouraging word and a warm hug. It pained me to hear about a recurring dream she had when she was younger:

I'm standing at the bottom of the staircase in my childhood home. No one else is around. It's eerily dark and quiet — still, but not peaceful. All of a sudden, a huge boulder comes around the corner and starts tumbling down the stairs, heading right for me. I stretch out my arms to catch the massive rock and then repeatedly try to fling it back up. I never get it back up the stairs.

I figured out a while ago that the dream is about fear. No one is around because when I'm anxious, I usually feel like I'm alone — carrying the weight of everyone's, including my own, impossible expectations. I may try to cast off my worries (or throw them back up the stairs in this case), but I never quite make it. That stupid boulder is too heavy, too awkward, maybe even too familiar.

The house is dark and quiet because when I'm truly afraid, I can't see God's light or hear God's voice. And even though nothing major may be happening in my life at that moment (things are "still"), I feel ill at ease, unsettled.

As God helped me process the dream, I realized that what I fretted about most were things that were ultimately out of my control, like what other people thought of me, past mistakes, my family, and work.

I've discovered two things, though: I can't hold it all together, and my life is in the hands of a God who loves me. Even people who don't claim to be Christians might use the phrase "it's in God's hands." But *my* life is not in the grasp of some impersonal, far-off, distant "god." The living God loves me, so much that He wants me to take all my worries to Him. That truth revolutionized my life and continues to do so.

It takes discipline for me not to fear the unknown, not to try to control what I ultimately know I can't. Sometimes I give in to worry. But when I take my thoughts to Him, the peace

He promises *is* there (see Isaiah 26:3; Philippians 4:6-7). That's world-changing, if you ask me.

The Suffering, Troubled, and Distracted Mind

I felt compelled to share all three of these stories with you because they reveal different levels of worry, fear, and anxiety. Not every woman deals with panic attacks like Tina does, but nineteen million American adults do suffer from clinical anxiety disorder.[1] Since women are twice as likely as men to experience fear that interferes with daily life (and because some psychologists posit that statistic would be significantly higher if everyone were medically evaluated),[2] I believe Tina's story will strike a chord with many.

Julia deals with a more common form of worry: a daily, sort of nagging concern for the details of life. I'll bet a huge number of women can relate to her sometimes annoying but very real concerns about things such as health, money, career, singleness or marriage, family, friends, and spirituality.

And Kara, though she never experienced panic attacks, did battle with recurrent, deep-seated fear. Like Kara, many women often report that their greatest anxieties concern out-of-control circumstances or "the unknown." They may dream about failure or loss; they suspect it will hit them anytime. Sometimes women plan and manipulate every detail of their lives, desperately trying to avoid the things they fear.

Tina, Julia, and Kara are not alone. *Lots* of women live fearful, anxious, or worried lives. We worry about everything from whether or not we left the coffeepot on to whether we'll *ever* get married or have children. We fret about what we eat, what we wear, and whether we'll live up to our potential. We can even worry ourselves sick. Medical professionals agree that anxiety leads to negative health problems, from increased blood pressure and heart rate to major depression, substance abuse, and even death.

In order to get a handle on worry, fear, and anxiety, I thought it would help to start by defining our terms. Both secularly and biblically, the words carry the same basic meaning: "the condition of being drawn mentally in different directions, [a] distraction of mind";[3] "painful agitation in the presence of or anticipation of danger";[4] "apprehensive uneasiness of mind, usually over an impending or anticipated ill . . . often marked by self-doubt about one's capacity to cope with it . . . suffering of mind; a troubled or engrossed state of mind."[5]

In other words, when I experience worry, fear, or anxiety, my brain is freaking out because of *something*. Whether that something is real or imagined, I anticipate that what happens next will be awful, painful, dangerous, threatening. The word *dread* comes to mind.

Though fear often motivates us to act, it almost never motivates us positively. It usually leads us to despair or to a frantic attempt at control. Neither of these reactions helps us grow in faith, hope, and love.

There are over three hundred references to fear in the Bible.[6] That's one for almost every single day of the year. I don't think this is a coincidence. In Matthew 6:34, Christ urges His beloved ones, "So do not worry about tomorrow, for tomorrow will bring worries of its own. Today's trouble is enough for today" (NRSV).

Life overflows with things that trigger anxiety. Every day I am confronted with the choice to worry or to trust. When I choose to fear, I take my eyes off the Author and Perfecter of my faith (see Hebrews 12:1-2). I focus on my problem, and my primary thought becomes either, *Do something! Get things back under control!* or *Run! Avoid! Lie down and give up!*

Though I have seen God carry me through troublesome situations over and over again, with each new set of fears, I often suspect that this time I won't make it, this time God won't be big enough or strong enough to pull me through. I may not consciously state, "You can't help me through this, Lord," but when it all boils down, that is, of course, what my anxiety declares.

So let's try to unpack the toxic beliefs that poison our minds when we entertain worry. Let's expose the false notions we live out when we allow our anxious, fearful minds to wander.

How Many Times Have You Thought, If Only . . . or What If . . . ?

I once heard that worry causes us to regret the past and fear the future. How tragically true I have found this to be. And what bondage! Worry robs the present of our presence, for we are ever living behind or ahead of ourselves. Joylessness and discouragement usually follow.

Let's look first at the "if only" myth.

LIE 1: If only . . .

How often I have despaired about my past, wondering whether making a different decision would have radically changed the course of my life. For some reason, I assume that everything would have been *better* if only I had done/thought/been _____. I don't consider as often that a different decision might have produced more negative effects in my life. My imagined response or action is almost always better than what I said or did.

When the onslaught of "if only" comes at me, I have to keep the truth in mind.

TRUTH 1: *I can trust God with my past, present, and future.*

In Isaiah 43:18-19, we read these words from God:

> "Do not remember the former things,
> or consider the things of old.
> I am about to do a new thing;
> now it springs forth, do you not perceive it?
> I will make a way in the wilderness
> and rivers in the desert." (NRSV)

I recognize that it is incredibly difficult to forget "the former things." I often fail to see the good in the moment, to perceive the "new thing" springing forth, because my eyes are trained backward, lamenting over what could have or should have been.

But look with me at the second half of verse 19: "I will make a way in the wilderness and rivers in the desert." What this says to me is that even if I completely flub up and make the worst possible decision, God will make a way. Not only that, He will bring life out of the deadliest of my choices. I can trust God with my past, present, and future; He is always doing a new thing.

I'll be the first to confess, however: It's a lot easier for me to trust when I *see* evidence of someone's trustworthiness. Fortunately for me (and you), God more than provides proof of His reliability. I'll give you an example. For quite some time, I wondered what would have happened if I had decided to attend Yale. As a seventeen-year-old, desperate to validate myself and impress others with success, honor, and achievement, I wanted to go to Yale more than anything. I got accepted, but my parents told me they could not afford to send me there. I cried, seriously contemplated joining the Navy ROTC program, and then decided to go to Rice.

I didn't want to go to Rice, despite the fact that my mom conveniently left articles around the house that praised it as the "Ivy of the South." She told me Rice had been rated twelfth in the nation when evaluated for academics, opportunities, and other things that I can't even remember (at the time I was neither interested in nor impressed by stats about or propaganda for Rice).

Finally, after waiting until the last possible second on April 30, I sent my acceptance postcard to Houston, the home of Rice University. But when I struggled with loneliness and emptiness and unfulfillment in my first year of college, I thought long and hard, *What if I were in New Haven right now?* At the time, I couldn't see the "new thing" God was bringing forth. I did not see a way. I felt the heat of the desert, and Yale appeared to have the water for which I thirsted.

Then God opened my eyes. I saw the first truly godly friendship I'd ever had grow in Texas, not Connecticut. I saw that I could graduate in three years — a way out. And though I did not know it at the time, graduating early enabled me to cross paths with my husband. Because Jeramy left California the month after I would have graduated from college had I taken the traditional four-year track, it would have been virtually impossible for us to meet and develop a relationship in that time frame.

Does this mean that if I had attended Yale, not Rice, I would not have met a kindred-spirited woman who cared for me and helped me grow? Would I have missed my chance to marry a godly man like Jeramy? Not necessarily. God is able. Nothing is too difficult for Him (see Luke 18:27 and Jeremiah 32:17, two awesome promises of God).

The point is not so much whether or not I made the "right" decision but whether I (and you) choose to see God's presence in every choice.

When I look at "if onlys," I can choose to remember His faithfulness, or I can worry. Depending on how spiritually alive I am on any given day, I choose one path or the other. But even when I worry for a season (which may be a *long* season), He reveals how He has made — indeed *is making* — a way for me.

LIE 2: What if . . . ?

What if I get hit by a car and have to stop working because of severe injuries? What if I just drove into the median or into oncoming traffic? (Come on, you know you've had that thought.) *What if I gain tons of weight? What if I get breast cancer? What if I never get married? What if my husband has an affair?*

The list of "what if" worries is never-ending. And the Enemy can torment us (or we can torment ourselves) with these thoughts quite effectively because some of our "what ifs" may, in fact, happen.

Satan uses "what if" thoughts, lying to us by saying that God doesn't care about us enough and that He isn't good enough or strong enough to get us through the worst things that may occur.

Women also sometimes think they don't deserve what they have — a healthy body, a good job, or a godly spouse and children. Whether because of past sin or general insecurity, many women fear that what they enjoy will be snatched from their hands by a pernicious, exacting, "you reap what you sow" God.

"What if" thinking calls into question the character of God.

For me, another major component of "what if" thinking involves fear of the unknown. I love the comment Anna Sewell makes in *Black Beauty*: "I am never afraid of what I know."[7] The unknown makes me feel out of control (which I am) and vulnerable (which I also am). I completely agree with psychologist Gregg Jantz, who notes, "Few things are as frightening as losing control, feeling powerless against overwhelming forces."[8]

Life is an overwhelming force. Relationships are an overwhelming force. Even God is an overwhelming force. I do *not* like feeling out of control or powerless, and the truth found in Ecclesiastes 7:14 doesn't really comfort me: "A man cannot discover anything about his future."

I sometimes try to make plans for how I would deal with certain trials. But even when a bad thing I've anticipated actually happens, the situation does not always go as I envisioned. Life, people, and an infinite number of potentialities make it impossible to discern what might happen.

Great. Thanks. Now what?

TRUTH 2: " 'There is hope for your future,' declares the LORD."[9]
Let me assure you: Though we are vulnerable and life is out of control, we are not powerless. On the contrary, we have the greatest power conceivable within us — the very Spirit of the living God. Yet this power is not ours to wield. The Spirit cannot be controlled, and we are called to submit to His movement. His work is out of our control. Even this can be pretty scary, if you ask me. I want to believe that I have control of *some* things, especially my future.

But God, who invites you and me to trust that He will make a way in the desert, also promises to guide us through that which is to come. Trusting God does not mean we are certain everything will be just grand all the time. We might experience many wonderful things, but in this broken world, we will also have trouble. Even this, however, does not have to discourage us. Jesus says, "I have told you all this so that you may have peace in me. Here on earth you *will* have many trials and sorrows. But take heart, because I have overcome the world" (John 16:33, NLT, emphasis added).

This is Truth.

Hebrews 6:18-19 states that "it is impossible for God to lie" (verse 18) and that hope is "a sure and steadfast anchor of the soul" (verse 19, NRSV). God cannot lie, so when He proclaims there is hope for your future, He speaks truth. And the hope He promises is an anchor — secure, firm, unwavering.

Of course, believing this truth requires that you concede God cannot lie. This takes us back to one of our most fundamental questions: What kind of God do you and I serve?

The living God assures us that

> *He doesn't treat us as our sins deserve,*
> *nor pay us back . . . for our wrongs. (Psalm 103:10, MSG)*

Would He take away what you have or withhold from you because you don't deserve it? No!

Our Lover proclaims,

> *"The mountains may depart*
> *and the hills be removed,*
> *but my steadfast love shall not depart from you,*
> *and my covenant of peace shall not be removed,*
> *says the LORD, who has compassion on you."*
> *(Isaiah 54:10, NRSV)*

The worst that life can throw at you — the actualization of your most awful "what if" thoughts — will not take His steadfast love, compassion, or peace from you.

Our minds need to be just as active, alive, and conscious to worry as they are to exercise faith. Why don't we start the rewarding journey toward using our vivid imaginations to hope and to have faith in the Anchor of our souls?

LIE 3: *If I don't control my circumstances, no one will.*

Do you ever fear that if you let go, you'll feel yourself spinning into chaos, toward failure, down into nothingness? Have you ever thought, *I trust God, but . . .* or *God is sovereign over everything except . . .* ? Perhaps you've had thoughts like these:

- I trust God, but I've disobeyed too long; I'd better get things cleaned up so I can give Him control of my life again.

- God is sovereign over everything except the bad things I or other people disobediently choose.

- I trust God, but He also asks me to take responsibility for my mistakes and even for the good things in my life.

We make loopholes like these in many of God's promises. But when we poke holes in the truth of God's sovereignty, we undermine His character in seriously destructive ways.

Maybe you've wondered whether God is really sovereign. I think every woman questions God's goodness at some point, whether due to tragedy in her own life or in the lives of others. And I think the fact that we don't believe we or the people we care about should have to suffer causes us to doubt the sovereignty of God.

I also believe that when we say that we fear losing control, many of us mean, "I fear feeling pain. If I can keep things tightly ordered, I won't have to face my wounds or the heartache of others." Being out of control doesn't feel safe. So we try to control our little worlds in order to avoid being hurt.

But, as a longtime control freak, I can attest to the truth that life *always* resists my attempts at total control. I can order my schedule and my routines — even, to some measure, my relationships. But something inevitably happens (and usually pretty quickly) that reminds me once again how little I can do to avoid pain, even in minor forms such as inconvenience and irritation.

TRUTH 3: *Only God has the power to bring* all *things under His control.*

Philippians 3:21 tells us that Yahweh has "power that . . . enables him to make all things subject to himself" (NRSV). God refers to Himself as "Sovereign Lord" 303 times in the Bible.[10] In 1 Timothy 6:15, God describes Himself as "the blessed and only Sovereign" (NRSV). Do you think He wants to make a point by consistently using this name for Himself?

We cannot control all things. Only God can. When life spins out of control, God reminds me of this truth. He also invites me to lean in and listen to Him as I ask, "What are the pain and fear telling me?"

In *Son of Laughter*, Frederick Buechner's retelling of the life of Jacob, people call God, "The Fear." At first I thought, *How awful! I know I'm supposed to fear the Lord, but to know Him as fear?* Then I discovered that The Fear is actually a Hebrew name for God. This is why it is safe to listen to fear, to lean in to pain. He is there.

God reveals His love for us through our battles with anxiety and worry. He calls to us from within, eager to teach, love, and deliver us. As He shows us that His faithfulness is real and affirms His care for us, we love Him more. We also learn from fear what we really value and what we may be investing too much concern in.

Vine's Expository Dictionary of New Testament Words defines *fear of God*, in part, as that which "banishes the terror that shrinks from His presence."[11] I'm sure we'd all concede, even if it took a little convincing, that the earthly things we fret about would shrink in God's presence. Consequently, instead of being one more thing to be anxious about, the fear of God actually drives out the worries that harass us.

The Fear banishes our anxiety; in His presence other worries shrink. Our minds and characters can be defined by trust in The Fear, whose Spirit is alive and at work in us.

I urge you to lean in to the pain. Listen. Watch. Anticipate His answer. Like Jacob, wrestle and do not let go until He blesses you (if you haven't yet, read about this in Genesis 32:22-31).

LIE 4: *If I don't worry about someone or something, I must not care enough.*

Even in church circles, worry has become an accepted — and expected — part of life. We often assume that if people *don't* worry (about their families, their spiritual state, their unsaved friends or colleagues, and so on), they must not care that much.

Women also think, *If I show God how much I care about someone, He won't let anything bad happen, right?*

Not even Webster agrees with this idea. Look with me at two definitions of *worry*:

1. To torment oneself with disturbing thoughts

2. To seize by the throat with teeth and shake or mangle, as one animal does another, or to harass by repeated biting and snapping[12]

How lovingly concerned does this make a worrier sound?

I confess that when I fear for someone else's safety or position, when I feel anxious about or threatened by something, my worry is usually more about me than it is about the thing or person that makes me concerned. *I* wouldn't want to face financial strain if Jeramy were unemployed, even though it would certainly affect him more than me. *I* don't want to face the death of one of my family members, even though he or she would be promoted to glory. Anxiety torments the worrier because it is really about the worrier. Fear seizes us by the throat and mangles us. Worry harasses, repeatedly bites, and disturbs us because, again, we don't want to face our own pain or the pain of others.

TRUTH 4: *God cares for my loved ones and my life more than I can.*

First Peter 5:7 instructs, "Let him have all your worries and cares, for he is always thinking about you and watching everything that concerns you" (TLB). "Give all your worries and cares to God, for he cares about what happens to you" (NLT). "Live carefree before God; he is most careful with you" (MSG).

He is watching out for you — indeed, for everything that even *concerns* you. Your God is always thinking about you. How reassuring!

It's important for me to note that one cannot "cast all [her] anxiety" (NRSV) on the Lord in one glorious moment. I have attempted this many times. I pray something such as, "Lord, I cast all of my worry about money on you." I feel great until that day's mail comes and I see that my electric bill has doubled.

I have found that a moment-by-moment exchange of my misconceptions for truth is the only solution to the problem of anxiety. A fear crops up, a repeated worry rears its head again, and right then I let God have *that* concern, "for he cares about what happens to [me]."

Worry, fear, and anxiety will continue to challenge us as long as we remain in this world. But we have the amazing opportunity to toss all our troubles upon Him who will care for and love — more than we ever could — everything and everyone who concerns us.

What Can I Do?

- **Admit that worry accomplishes nothing.** In the book of Matthew, Jesus asks, "Who of you by worrying can add a single hour to his life?" (6:27). I know the answer is no one. But I often live under the false assumption that I can solve my own problems. Today I come clean: I have never fixed anything by worrying about it. My anxiety over paying an extra $150 to repair my radiator (does that thing really matter, anyway?) does not transform my bill at the mechanic's. I know there may be those of you who will dismiss this thought by claiming, "But worrying about _____ leads me to act." Maybe it does. But worry need not be the force that motivates you. If you recall with me, anxiety is a suffering of mind and a troubled state of thinking. Suffering and trouble aren't the most positive reasons to do or be something. Instead of drawing us to something or someone out of genuine love, fear drives us to make our own way and protect ourselves. And doing so can prevent us from seeing God's caring provision for us. I don't ever want to miss out on seeing His hand move. And I don't want to waste my time trying to add a single hour to my life by worrying.

- **Show up in God's presence.** Sometimes we fear even to approach God because we mistakenly believe that He will scold us for being worried. But we cannot cast our anxiety on Jesus unless we are near Him. The Lord gently assures us,

> *"Do not fear, for I am with you,*
> *do not be afraid, for I am your God;*
> *I will strengthen you, I will help you,*
> *I will uphold you with my victorious right hand."*
> *(Isaiah 41:10, NRSV)*

In the brilliant light of the Prince of Peace, who cares for you and everything that concerns you, the things we worry about don't shine so brightly. Most of the time, this doesn't happen for me instantaneously. For me, the process of casting my anxiety on Him takes time, quiet, and repeating the truth over and over. But all this happens as I am with God, drawing close to Him and asking Him to draw near to me. When I show up, I always find that He is waiting to receive me with arms wide open.

- **Lean on others.** When things stay in my mind, they often grow larger than life. When I confess my anxiety, however, I find that just verbalizing my worry helps tame it, making it seem smaller. The Bible tells us, "Worry weighs a person down; an encouraging word cheers a person up" (Proverbs 12:25, NLT). We need the help of other people. Moreover, we need the help of the One who can bear the weight of all our concerns. My heart resonates with the words of Jo Kadlecek, who confesses, "Even when I am afraid and a huge part of me wants to run and hide—alone—it does not take long to see how utterly needy I am for a power grander than my ego, a mind wiser than my own, a compass better than my emotion. And a lot of friends along the way."[13] This is true for all of us. When fear, anxiety, and worry grip you, lean on those closest to you—your loving Lord and your trusted friends.

- **Don't be discouraged when fears reassert themselves.** Recurrent fears are merely part of the human condition. When worries crop up again, they diminish our memory of God's faithfulness. But troubles need not extinguish the memory of God's care. When fear knocks on the door of our thoughts—yet again—we can return to the consuming fire of God's everlasting love (no matter how small our flame of faith flickers at any given moment). He can and will remind us (see John 14:26-27).

*Most loving Father, whose will it is for us to give thanks
for all things, to fear nothing but the loss of you, and to
cast all our care on you who cares for us: Preserve me
from faithless fears and worldly anxieties, that no clouds
of this mortal life may hide from me the light of that
love which is immortal, and which you have manifested
to us in your son Jesus Christ our Lord; who lives and
reigns with you, in the unity of the Holy Spirit, one God,
now and for ever. Amen.*[14]

On That Thought . . .

1. Which of the three women who shared their stories at the
    beginning of this chapter do you relate to most? Why?

2. What do you think about God's name The Fear? How does the
    advice to "listen to fear, to lean in to pain" hit you?

3. Write down the five things you are most concerned about.
    Whether you consider them small or major things, take enough
    time to identify the lies that may have contributed to unhealthy
    worry, fear, or anxiety about each of them. Through prayer, invite
    God to enable you to cast your cares on Him.

4. Take one of your "what if" or "if only" thoughts to the very end.
    (Examples: If you are single, *What if I never get married?* If you are
    married, *What if my husband leaves me?*) What fears are at the very
    end of your thoughts? What lies about who you are and who God
    is do you find?

5. What is the hindrance that most often keeps you from showing up in God's presence? How might you begin to overcome that obstacle?

CHAPTER 4

ONE MORE THING

Seeking the Greatest Desire

There are two ways to get enough. One is to continue to accumulate more and more, the other is to desire less.

G. K. CHESTERTON

If you met my girlfriend Brita, you might wonder why she would envy anyone. Brita is a statuesque blonde with killer legs, striking blue eyes, and an amazing singing voice. She grew up in a gorgeous and affluent area of the country with a family who had resources and love to spare, and she later graduated from a prestigious college with a variety of vocal and stage successes under her belt. Brita is currently dating a handsome and dynamic man who thinks she's one of the most generous, considerate, beautiful women on the planet. He glows with love for her. Some might say she's got it all.

Yet Brita confessed to me that she envies — deeply and regularly.

In response to my question, "What do you envy most?" Brita mentioned two things: beauty and faith. I asked her to expound on her envy of appearance first. She said, "Everybody's obsessed with beauty, and everyone's telling you how you should look. It's difficult not to size yourself up against other people. While I don't think I'm unattractive, I know I don't look like the Hollywood glamour girls with their cute little features and their perfect skin."

Brita mentioned the names of some women she thought of as extremely attractive, including a couple of her friends. I posed the question, "Do you think they envy anyone or anything?" She replied, "Well, it's probably not someone else's *looks* that they envy. Maybe they're jealous of people's lives—of their families, their marriages, their happiness."

Brita paused.

"But, you know, when I think about it, even the most gorgeous of my friends compare themselves with other people and complain about their appearance. I guess you can never be pretty enough. Still, I sometimes wonder what it would be like if I were extremely, extremely attractive."

So Brita and I discussed for a moment what she thought would happen if she got the look she envied. She said, "I think I'd be more content . . . and happier. On days when I feel good about how I look, I find I'm more fun to be around. So if I always felt good about how I looked, people would enjoy being around me more, and that would make me happy."

At this point we transitioned into talking about her envy of faith. Brita started: "I don't see myself as a very good Christian. I look at other believers, and they seem to have a more dynamic walk with Christ. They're serving, they're godlier, they have better prayer lives. I want that, too. Even though I lead worship now and then, I often feel disconnected from my church and sometimes from God. I envy the Christians my age who plug into small groups, who attend all the twentysomething activities. They seem more satisfied with life. And then I wonder, *If I were closer to God and helping more people, would I still be obsessed with my looks?* I definitely wouldn't have as much time to worry about it."

She laughed. A genuine, honest, yearning laugh.

"So what would it mean if you never got what you envied?" I asked. "What if your appearance never changed? Try to go to the very end of your thoughts, Brita. What would it *really* mean?"

"If people don't like my look now and it never changed, I might not be good enough to get cast as an actress, which is what I've dreamed of doing since I was a little girl. If I couldn't live out my passion, then I'm afraid my life wouldn't have meaning. I would feel worthless and unimportant."

I pressed in, "And what if you never became the kind of Christian you think you should be?"

"If I didn't become as good a Christian as the people I admire, I wouldn't be as close to God, which would make me less likely to really live out my faith. And what would be the point of life if I'm not even a good Christian? I'd doubt my worth because I wouldn't be doing anything eternally significant. I'd feel like I wasn't good enough — even for God.

"Envying like this never makes me feel better. When I dwell on what I don't have, what I am not, I tend to get frustrated, even angry. And then I feel discouraged and hopeless and fearful.

"Pining after any one thing also makes me less content with other things in my life. I start to wonder why I can't have enough money to fix up a cute apartment or buy a new car. I know these things aren't ultimately that important. But knowing that doesn't stop the desire for just one more thing."

The Lie of "One More Thing"

One more thing. The one thing that will bring happiness and fulfillment. The one change in my appearance that will make me like *her*. The one aspect of my faith that will make it as alive as *hers*. Just one more thing and then I'll be satisfied.

We envy status. We envy position. We envy the bodies of other women. We envy the tenderness of their boyfriends or husbands. We envy the money a friend has to blow on matching shoes for every one of her designer outfits. We even envy spiritual gifts. *If only I could sing* [or dance or teach or pray] *like she does*, we think, *then I'd be . . .*

What? What would you be? Would you be happy? Would you be fulfilled?

I doubt it. A new envy almost always waits on the other side of "one more thing." The crazy part is, this reality continues to shock us. If Brita decided to get, say, a nose job, how easy would it be for her to start obsessing about another part of her body? If you got the new car (or carpet or purse or man) you've been longing for, do you really believe you would be satisfied — forever?

Even as we mature in Christ and reorder our priorities, envy often surprises us, catches us off guard. Brita wants to be a better Christian, and she wants to use her gifts and talents in the field she's felt drawn to since childhood. These are not bad things. Yet even if we desperately want a good thing — a husband or a child, for instance — if we let desire turn bitter, we steal from ourselves.

When we give in to its lure, envy forces us down a scary, endless spiral. We will always be able to find another person with some quality or possession that arouses in us dissatisfied and resentful longings. Jealousy and greed filch our resources (how much money have we spent trying to acquire the "right" stuff?). And envy sucks our spirits dry, robbing us of joy and energy.

Consuming jealous desire will sap the life right out of you, as Proverbs 14:30 powerfully expresses:

> *Peace of mind means a healthy body.*
> *But jealousy will rot your bones.* (NCV)

Envy also devours our longing for Who and what actually bring us the life we crave — namely Jesus and His righteousness. The Lord speaks to this clearly: "Where you have envy and selfish ambition, there you will find disorder and every evil practice" (James 3:16).

If given the choice between a healthy body or a rotting one, a disordered life or a peacefully content one, there'd be no question what every woman would choose. When asked whether she wanted to pursue Jesus or evil, again, there'd be no contest. Yet despite having been robbed by envy before, so many of us continue to run after that "one more thing."

Like Brita, we see women around us who have stronger faith or more beautiful faces and bodies. They get the guys, they get the acclaim, they get it all. *What's wrong with me?* we wonder. We don't have all we want — or think we want. Why? Isn't something amiss if what we desire does not translate into what we receive?

Questions like these open the door for the lies of envy. And all too often, our jealous thoughts are joined by an uninvited and undesirable companion to envy — greed. What heinous words envy and greed are. In my mind, these terms invoke images of little green monsters, hoarding every good thing for themselves and stealing the joy of others. Sadly, these mental pictures are not far from the truth. Both envy and greed reduce us. These sins wrap us up in *our* desires and often what we perceive as *our* needs. Whether our longings are for good things or bad, whether our motivations are selfless or selfish, dwelling with unholy desire on what another has or is causes us to become less than what God created us to be.

The media promotes greed and envy by continually reminding us that we do not have it all. And when others seem to have more than we do, our yearning for things and for happiness quickly turns to envy. Yet advertisements selectively parcel up people's lives and present only the positive aspects. We see a woman driving a fully loaded BMW, laughing with her boyfriend at whatever seems to have caught their fancy. But what we *don't* see is that she lives in a studio apartment because of her nine-hundred-dollar-a-month car payment. We also don't learn that she hasn't spoken to her parents in five years and that the man she's with is having an affair with another woman. We envy and lust greedily after her life when we see her through the microscopic lens of a sporty car and a pleasant moment.

The only thing marketers never reveal is that you *can't* have it all.

Historically, envy and greed ranked as two of the worst human failings (both were included on Pope Gregory's list of the seven deadly sins). Today, greed and envy are almost assumed. Costco sells a wine named Seven Deadly Sins, and a salon near my house calls itself Envy.

What's the message here? That envy and greed are not deadly sins but enticing, attractive, and desirable options.

According to Mary Ellen Ashcroft,

> *In our society we may parrot "In God We Trust"; but the reality is "In Things We Trust." That's how we live. A society that has lost a genuine belief in God doesn't become godless; it designs other gods for itself. In a society that no longer really believes in God, materialism becomes our religion. Shopping is the worship and sacrament of the religion materialism.*[1]

We often live envious, greedy, discontented lives even though we know Christ came to bring us abundant life (see John 10:10). We greedily buy what we have envied, thinking primarily of ourselves. We rationalize that we need something simply because we want it. Buying and consuming also give us a sense of control over our lives, our homes, our future. If we have what we want, we will be happy and fulfilled, right?

Greed causes us to fear that what we have will be taken from us. So along with grabbing for ourselves, we become stingy, withholding and hoarding our things. And then we envy those who seem free with their money and whose financial wells don't appear to be running dry. Envy and greed often cause us to push others away as well. We begin to perceive people as competitors for or threats to what we want.

Consider the times you've been struck with envy or greed. I recall the physical reactions in my body on such occasions: tension, increased heart rate, sometimes a feeling that I'll implode unless I do something — *now*. These physiological responses mirror those that occur when we're faced with a genuine threat (such as a physical attack). They are often called our "fight or flight" impulses. But not getting what we want is not a genuine threat. It only appears to be so.

And while we're talking about some uncomfortably close aspects of jealousy and greed, let's try this one on for size: We often want to *be envied.* We secretly hope that someone will think *we've* got the best-decorated apartment or the hottest boyfriend/fiancé/husband (even though we *really* want our friends to admire his godliness, right?).

We may not immediately recognize it, and — whether due to shame or a lack of desire to change — few of us ever acknowledge it, but when we greedily buy and hoard, it's often because deep down we lust for the envious approval of others. The lie of *If someone envies me, some part of my life must be "good enough,"* creeps into our subconscious.

If someone thinks my outfit is the cutest or my body is the most attractive, if another person is sinfully consumed with jealousy for something I have, it must mean *I* did something right: *I* bought the clothes that someone else really wants; *I* worked out the hardest and ate the healthiest. *I* matter; *I'm* good — at least at something.

The great thieves envy and greed consequently steal the strength of our relationships on top of the life, peace, and holiness they've already purloined. We cannot love others when we long to be envied. If we care more about being validated for what we do, have, or look like, we often drag others into the black hole of jealousy and avarice with us.

Eventually, envy and greed will leave us empty-handed and lonely, loveless and lifeless. So as we analyze the lies that cause us to crave what we don't have and then keep on pining for more, let's keep this in mind: The true threat is not that we won't have what we want but that envy and greed will devour us — and everything we truly love.

When Is It "Good Enough"?

LIE 1: *If I don't have _____ (or am not _____), I'm not good enough.*

Brita so vulnerably revealed this deception in her own thinking. She admitted to me her fears: If she didn't have a flawless look, she wasn't good enough to be an actress. If she wasn't as good a Christian as other people, she wouldn't be good enough for God. If she didn't do what she loved or enjoy the kind of relationship with God that others seemed to have, her life would be a waste.

Unfulfilled longings bring up questions like these: *Am I not good enough for what I want? Is God punishing me for something I've done or withholding from me because of something I haven't done? What's wrong with me?*

The world tells us something is amiss if we don't have what we want — a cute husband, the latest fashions, a stylish car, a gorgeous figure, the most prestigious position, and so forth. The message is clear: You must fight to get these things, because having them means you are worth something and are in control. Without things, without accomplishments, without beauty, you are nothing. Truth teaches us differently.

Truth 1: *I am not the sum of what I own or accomplish.*

God does not love a beautiful woman or a woman who has a yacht more than a woman who recycles aluminum cans to support herself. God does not favor those who graduate Phi Beta Kappa and withhold blessing from those who struggle with learning disabilities. God does not prefer mothers to lawyers or married women to singles — or vice versa. God never asks whether you are good enough. He decided that long ago.

The *only* answer to nagging questions of self-worth is an intimate relationship with Jesus Christ. No amount of money, no abundance of things will assure you that you are good enough, nor will any number of stunning achievements. No degree of beauty or power of position will satisfy forever your longing to be valued, to be good enough.

In abandoned, sacrificial love, God declared at Calvary and declares eternally, "In me, you are good enough — just as you are."

The world will continue to lie to you. Ads will still attempt to deceive you into believing that unless you look like X or have Y, you are nothing. But by God's grace you have the right to proclaim, "No matter what I have or do, I am good enough."

LIE 2: *If I have _____, I'll be happy and fulfilled.*

Even if you believe in your eternal acceptability to God (though many of us do not trust in this truth enough to actually live it out), you may not take joy and find satisfaction in what He's given you here on earth.

Sometimes we feel this only to a small degree. For instance, the black shoes I purchased seven years ago recently began to show a lot of wear. I put them in a bag with some other clothes I wanted to donate and dropped them off at Goodwill.

A few weeks later, having forgotten that I gave them away, I frantically searched for them, eager to complete the look I wanted. Of course, they were nowhere to be found. I showed up for church late and frustrated. (I know you must think I am a complete heathen for making my family late for worship, all because I wanted to wear the right shoes. You'd never do that, right?)

For a week, I could not stop thinking about buying a new pair of black shoes. Even during my prayer time, I felt distracted by images of all the outfits that would be ruined if I didn't have black shoes. I tried to repent of my silly, greedy craving (didn't I have more pairs of shoes than 90 percent of women around the world?), but I could not shake the thoughts.

So I went shopping, thinking if I just found the shoes, the unrest within me would quiet. I tried on several pairs; most made me look like the Wicked Witch of the West.

After an eight-day pursuit, I finally found some black shoes that fit and that I liked, so I bought them. But when I tried to walk any distance in them, even when I stood for an extended period of time, my feet ached for hours. So I stored the shoes — with a snarl — under my bed.

I never thought the black shoes would bring me *ultimate* satisfaction, but I certainly thought they would bring me relief from gnawing desire. They did not — not merely because the shoes were uncomfortable, but also because next to the faded black clothes in my closet, they looked shockingly out of place. Now I needed new pants!

Though I wasn't expecting my new shoes to keep me satisfied forever, there are things we envy or covet or hoard because deep down we suspect they will bring us enough satisfaction to really last. As singles, we envy happy couples because we believe if we could only get married, we wouldn't feel empty anymore. Yet married women often envy the freedom and independence of singles, sometimes despairing in a relationship that doesn't meet all of their expectations.

If, if, if.

Though many of us have been raised to believe that Christ is the only answer to the deepest ache in our hearts, we live out the lie that if we had just one more thing, we'd be content. But it's never enough. When, or if, we get what we long for, our greedy human hearts yearn for yet another "one more thing."

Truth 2: *Only Christ Himself brings ultimate satisfaction.*
The psalmist writes,

> *I have no one in heaven but you.*
>> *I want nothing on earth besides you.*
> *My mind and my body may become weak.*
>> *But God is my strength.*
> *He is mine forever. (73:25-26, NCV)*

> *You open Your hand*
> *And satisfy the desire of every living thing. (145:16, NASB)*

> *Only God "satisfies me with good things." (103:5, NCV)*

As wonderful as any thing or any person may be, earthly joys, accomplishments, acquisitions, and exaltations fade away — quickly.

Scientists proved long ago that left on its own and given enough time, the universe would dissolve into utter chaos. Faith aside, things last only so long. They break down, fall apart, and, in doing so, often disappoint us bitterly.

Our Creator spoke of the fragility of earthly things ages before science discovered entropy. Through the apostle John, God declared, "The world and all its wanting, wanting, wanting is on the way out — but whoever does what God wants is set for eternity" (1 John 2:17, MSG).

Getting what you envy or all that your greedy heart longs for may make you happy for a time. Having all that you've dreamed of may satisfy you while you dwell in this cruel, crazy, beautiful world. But in the end (or even next week), it will all fade away. Nothing lasts, no earthly pleasure or possession; only Jesus can sustain you and give you joy. To "make a clean sweep of . . . envy," as 1 Peter 2:1 (MSG) commands us to do, we must reject the lie that things will satisfy us. As we learn in Psalm 27:4-5, the only thing that brings eternal satisfaction is living in and with Christ:

> *The* one thing *I want from God, the* [one] thing *I seek most of all, is the privilege of meditating in his Temple, living in his presence every day of my life, delighting in his incomparable perfections and glory. There I'll be when troubles come. He will hide me. He will set me on a high rock.* (TLB, *emphasis added*)

With David, let us claim that we want not one thing more, but one thing *only*: the everlasting, rich, and fully satisfying presence of our Lord.

LIE 3: *What I want doesn't change what really matters to me.*

The Enemy would like us to believe that sin doesn't start until we *act* on the envy or greed that we feel. He whispers that what stays in our minds, what we dream about and long for, isn't sin unless we do something "bad" trying to acquire it.

The world confirms this message, and in a short time, we've embraced the deception so thoroughly that we can't even recognize its toxicity anymore. We convince ourselves, sometimes even without the Devil's help, *I'm not doing anything wrong. Besides, this is the only way I can get that new* _____.

We spend more time envying a friend's new house, engagement ring, job, or spontaneously romantic relationship with her husband than we do asking *why* we long for those things. Yet envy and greed are only symptoms of a deeper hunger, a desire that speaks volumes about what is truly important to us.

Truth 3: *My desires tell me a great deal about my values.*
God wired us to desire so that we might seek Him (the object of all true desire), as well as discover the things He created for us to enjoy. Just because women sometimes experience unrighteous longing does not lead to the conclusion that we should never want.

Psalm 37:4 says,

> Take delight in the Lord,
>> and he will give you your heart's desires. (NLT)

Whether or not you've heard this verse before (or been frustrated because it hasn't seemed to be true of your life), stop with me for a moment and meditate on this remarkable promise.

First of all, God does not condemn desire. In fact, He seems ready, even excited, to give us what we truly long for. But something comes first: taking delight in Him. At one point in my life, after reading this verse, I believed that I wasn't living the life I wanted because I wasn't taking delight in the Lord. So I tried really hard to take delight in Him. But how much enjoyment and freedom comes with a relationship that is tenaciously driven? I can't simply grit my teeth and claw my way toward delight in God.

Rather than lamenting that we don't have what we want, often dwelling on feelings of jealousy or greed, we can learn to use each wave of desire as an opportunity to learn how to take delight in God and evaluate anew what is truly significant. Pulling apart what envy and greed really indicate about my life gives me the chance to ask God to sustain me and help me find my satisfaction in Him.

When I evaluate what I desire and *why* I crave it, I sometimes see that I've placed too high a value on a thing, a person, or a position. Sometimes I realize that I've wanted something more than I've wanted God. Envy and greed often show me that I've loved too much the things that matter little and loved too little the things that count for something. Do you think this might ever have been true of you?

Thank God that He can reverse that equation in us. Jesus draws us to spend time lavishly loving Him — learning how to enjoy Him, "waste" time with Him, and let thoughts of everything else become lost in the sea of His pleasure (aka taking delight in Him). But this is not always easy. And the second part of Psalm 37:4, "and he will give you your heart's desires" (NLT), can be confusing, not to mention incredibly difficult to believe. In essence, it claims, "Run after God and everything else will fall into the right place at the right time."

But I'll wager there are many women out there who would argue (as I once did), "How can He say that? I've been trying to follow God, trying to enjoy Him, and *nothing* that I really want has happened."

I wish I had the perfect answer for you, but I don't. The answer is definitely not, "Try harder; if you were really loving God you would have it." And it is also not, "Just wait; you'll have it eventually" or "You must want the wrong things; God will eventually take your desire away if He's not going to give it to you."

All of those answers (which I have heard or told myself at different points in my life) either leave us with despair over our own efforts to love God or lead to disappointment with Him. In many ways, God's ways seem mysterious (if we're honest, sometimes annoying) to us. But He has revealed some things very clearly.

Our God claims that He knows *everything* we desire, *always* wants what's best for us, and *thoroughly* understands when the right time is for us to have it. Do you believe that? The only way we can have confidence and live in the truth that Psalm 37:4 reveals about God and how He deals with our desires is by trusting that the Lord is who He says He is. That's easy, right?

No. Faith in God's goodness with respect to our desires may be (for many of us *will* be) difficult, especially if we do not receive the answers we hope for. But asking God, "Will you show me what my heart really desires?" and "Will you show me what matters much and what matters little?" is a good place to start.

The Lord doesn't want you to bury your desires any more than He wants you to lust after them. He wants to use your longings to teach you who He is and what matters most. God doesn't give us desires so that He can snatch them away from us and scold us for wanting something that is so meaningless. That is *not* our God.

Instead, He gives us desires because He longs to fulfill us. He aches to give us the things that will actually bring us delight and satisfaction. In order to do that, He may need to refine some of our wants (in the same way my parents had to help me see that it wasn't really a good idea to keep a raccoon for a pet).

We fall into envy and greed when we focus more on how much we yearn for something than we do on the Giver of desire and whether He says the thing we crave will make our lives fuller, more peaceful, and more enjoyable.

When you feel envious or greedy, ask God to reveal what this longing means in the greater scheme of your life. He knows, and He wants to help you deal with your desire rightly. The Spirit *will* help you discern between godly desire and sinful craving. He *will* show you the things that matter much and help you let go of those that matter little. Your job is simply to be willing to learn, to enjoy, and to agree with Him.

Lie 4: *If I don't grab hold of something, nothing will be left for me.*

When we believe that we attain things or positions because of our own hard work or savvy, we miss the Truth that we are *stewards* — not owners — of all God has given us.

The misconception that if I don't grab hold of something, nothing will be left for me stems from a fundamental misunderstanding of God's nature. We think that the good stuff God gives to others will somehow run out, that there won't be enough for us if we don't do something for ourselves. We believe that He shows favor only to those who have more than we do, and so we compete for the things we admire, long for, and covet. But these are toxic lies.

We also think that we deserve a fair shake, an even playing field, and even some perks along the way. When we're kids we want the exact same things our siblings have (or, if anyone is going to get them, we want the *bigger* and *better* ones). We go to the mall and think we deserve a good parking spot as much as anyone. Selfishness and hypocritical pride go into overdrive when we attempt to determine what's fair or what we deserve.

What do we really have coming to us? How much is our share? Does the world really revolve around a survival-of-the-fittest principle? If so, will there be enough for *us*?

TRUTH 4: *In Christ, nothing is in short supply.*

God gives bountifully; He gives without ceasing. James 1:17 tells us, "Every desirable and beneficial gift comes out of heaven" (MSG). There is no other source; there is no other fount of goodness.

Paul speaks of God meeting all our needs according to the "glorious riches in Christ Jesus" (Philippians 4:19). The trouble comes when we see our needs as synonymous with our wants and when we see our desires as our rights and dues.

God longs to give to you. Nothing is in short supply with Him. Cease your striving; do not compare or compete. Let your thoughts be ruled by the Truth that the generous, unlimited God you serve delights to bestow on you everything that matters — including an impossibly incredible and eternal inheritance (see Ephesians 1).

How wonderful that we can look forward to enjoying the abundance of heaven. We also, however, can realistically and righteously deal with the good things we want while we live on earth.

Sinful desires, cravings for things that go against the will of God, should be dismissed immediately (even though this is sometimes quite challenging). But what about the longing for things God may very well give us?

For instance, we know that being married or having a child does not ultimately matter in eternity. There are no husbands or families in heaven; but should we see those things as irrelevant here and now?

No way. Again, we cannot unreservedly deny or dwell on our desires. Finding a balance between acknowledging and obsessing about what we want is key to enjoying — here on earth — an authentic relationship with Christ and the full, lasting life He died to bring us.

Longing for any good thing that God may or may not give you in His perfect will and time (for example, a best friend, a husband and family, a reliable car, or a vacation to help you regroup and refresh) always gives us two options: be consumed or be captivated.

When we consistently choose to envy and greedily run after what we want, we fall into the pit of self-consumption and joyless existing. When we choose, however, to be captivated by our winsome, delightful God, we can lay our desires before Him (even when it would be less painful to deny that we want something than it would be to continue praying, "Lord, You know my heart; Thy will be done"). Captivated to our loving Lord, we can wait for the revelation of His will and the fulfillment of our hearts' true desires.

What Can I Do?

- **Consider the hidden costs.** Maybe you've heard the quip, "Women always want what they can't have, and when they get it they don't want it anymore." I think there's a lot of truth in this saying, as annoying as it may be when it applies to my life. Do we *really* want to look like a movie star and run the risk of relinquishing our privacy forever? Do we *really* desire to have a fancy car that costs more to maintain, repair, and insure than most of the world makes in a year? Do we *really* want to have to wonder if people like to be with us because of our money or our appearance? Do we *really* want to date the "sexiest man alive," knowing that women will constantly compete for his attention? Sometimes we think we want something, and we envy those who have it without considering the hidden costs of obtaining that which we desire. Take some time to discern whether what you want is worth the hidden costs.

- **Reorder your time.** Envy and greed suck time from that which truly matters. Because we long for a new dress, a new body, or a new car, we spend time working to acquire these things. We waste time coveting what others have. For many women, feelings that come after longingly perusing a catalog or fashion magazine (even a home and garden magazine) can become comparable to the lust incited by pornography. We want, we crave, we imagine ourselves having and holding. And left unattended, our envy and greed enslave us. Let's spend our time and energy on those things that promote life, not bondage.

- **Recognize the signs of envy and greed.** Very few of us think, *I'm going to pursue everything I want and envy everyone who has what I don't.* No. Envy and greed sneak up on us. We find ourselves in the thick of coveting things and wonder how in the world we got so far. Learning to watch for a few warning signals may help us nip envy and greed in the bud. Look out for times when you feel unable to rejoice over another's success or recent purchase. When you feel the urge to gossip about someone you think is wealthier, prettier, or more successful than you are, ask yourself why. Finally, evaluate feelings of entitlement — "I deserved that" or "That should have been mine." What do we really deserve?

- **Practice gratitude.** Elisabeth Elliot, who lost her husband to the Auca Indians in the land she had wanted to evangelize, writes,

"We accept and thank God for what is given, not allowing the *not-given* to spoil it."[2] We focus so often on the "not-given" that we ignore the many blessings of God. Psalm 103:2 declares,

> *Praise the LORD, O my soul,*
>   *and forget not all his benefits.*

"Don't forget a single blessing," as *The Message* puts it. As we practice gratitude, we find ourselves better equipped to put off envy and greed.

⁓

O merciful Creator, thy hand is open wide to satisfy
the needs of every living creature: Make us, we
beseech thee, ever thankful for thy loving providence;
and grant that we, remembering the account that we
must one day give, may be faithful stewards of thy
good gifts; through Jesus Christ our Lord, who with
thee and the Holy Spirit liveth and reigneth, one God,
for ever and ever. Amen.[3]

On That Thought . . .

1. What is the thing you envy most? Why do you think you desire it?

2. Who is the person you envy most? Do you want what he or she has or to be who he or she is? Why?

3. How do you think you would feel if you got what you've longed for? Why?

4. Which of the suggested ways to begin conquering envy and greed do you find the most difficult to imagine practicing? Why? Look for lies that have infiltrated your thinking. Write or say a prayer for God's help in starting to overcome envy and greed.

5. What does it mean to you to desire Christ and Christ alone? Write God a prayer that describes what you long for most. Ask Him to tell you what it looks like to crave Him. Listen. Write down what you hear.

6. How do you think God wants you to live in order to be more fully satisfied with Him? What might that look like?

CHAPTER 5

OFFENDED

Experiencing Genuine Forgiveness

The demands of forgiveness are so daunting that they seem humanly impossible. . . . Only reckless confidence in a Source greater than ourselves can empower us to forgive the wounds inflicted by others. . . . There is only one place to go — Calvary.

BRENNAN MANNING

When I first met Johnna at church, she looked harrowed and harassed. Her brow was constantly set in a scowl, and nothing in life seemed to satisfy her. I knew she had only recently come to know Jesus and that she had been wounded deeply (though at the time I did not know how). But, honestly, I didn't really want to be around her. She looked at life pessimistically and often spoke bitterly. In time, however, I watched Johnna transform. The light of life invaded her features. Love flowed out of her. Humble words replaced harsh ones. She wasn't perfect, but something was *different*. Later, I discovered how the gospel of reconciliation had changed her life. For the past decade, Jesus has been enabling Johnna to face what she sees as the most difficult challenge of her life: learning to forgive.

From Johnna

Twelve years old and happily relishing the freedom of summer vacation, I sat in my bedroom listening to the first CD I bought with my own money. The door slammed, and my parents started yelling (nothing new). Then my dad's voice faded.

The next time I saw my father was in divorce court. He was there with her — the woman he committed adultery with, the woman he abandoned us for. I already hated him, but my bitterness exploded at the sight of his mistress. I refused to talk to him. A few months later, Dad stopped asking if I would spend the weekend with him and his "new" family. I didn't speak with him again for ten years.

At twenty, I came to know Christ. Slowly, gently, Jesus started to open and heal the deep wounds of my father's betrayal. He asked me to make a choice; He invited me to forgive. I decided to call my dad on my twenty-third birthday. We're now trying to be friends.

My journey toward forgiveness started with a choice, but uncovering the far-reaching, devastating effects of unresolved hurt took, and continues to take, work — arduous, often painful effort.

As I've waged the battle in my mind between forgiveness and bitterness, I've seen the effects of choosing one path or the other.

When I allow bitter thoughts to grow and fester, I lose not only the smaller battle for that moment but a part of the greater battle for true life as well. I lose the joy of relationship. I lose spiritual footing. I lose hope. Withholding forgiveness is a losing battle.

Yet when I forgive, through God's mercy, I taste the sweetness of relationship. I feel strength in my spirit. I gain hope. The vinegar of bitterness within me used to sour everything. Now I know again the satisfaction and freedom of forgiveness.

Each day, I must remain vigilant, attuned to the state of my thoughts. Though my dad and I have agreed to start over, the memories aren't gone. But now, when I hear the toxic, deceiving words leading me down the path of unforgiveness, I ask God to help me resist temptation. I don't always allow Him to align my thoughts with His. Still, I'm pressing on, knowing that if I give in, resentment will eventually swallow me.

Through the process of forgiveness, God asks me to turn over *every* offense done to me, past or present. This doesn't happen overnight. I still have to school my mind in the belief that God is bigger than my hurt and bigger than the people who've hurt me. I must choose to cling to the truths that He makes all things new and works all things together for good (see Revelation 21:5; Romans 8:28).

Yet as I practice surrendering to God my desire to control and to get payback, I find the next offense and the one after that are easier to forgive. Thank God it doesn't always have to be as hard as it was the first time!

Which Option Will You Choose?

Years of stored-up hurts kept Johnna from experiencing the fullness of joy and the abundant life that Christ purchased for her with His blood (see John 10:10). She found that freedom lies not in restitution, nor even in her father's apologies and life changes, but in forgiving from her heart.

What pain do you continue to carry with you? Whose name do you cringe to hear, simply because the wound he or she inflicted on you was so deep that you feel unable to forget? Which offense do you remember so vividly that you can taste the disappointment, anger, and anguish as if it just happened?

Like many of you, I don't classify myself as a bitter or resentful person. But I have struggled to forgive on many levels. An influential woman in my life repeatedly made comments that stabbed me like mental daggers. A man I deeply respected betrayed his wife and young children. A friend I trusted stole money from my family and never admitted her wrong. And during many of those times, I didn't know what to do with my hurt.

In this fallen world, people *will* disappoint us. People *will* injure us. It's not a question of if as much as when. And it's also a matter of in what way and how deeply.

People can hurt us compulsively (over and over again, whether intentionally or not). They may wound us as the pain of their own injuries spills over into their relationships. They may offend us with their mistakes or because they think we deserve it. People may even harm us with their good intentions.

When someone wounds us, we have one of two options: We forgive, or we don't. That may sound simplistic, but there is simply no third option, no plan C.

Try as we may, we cannot shrug off or forget a true offense. We can allow minor infractions to roll off our backs, but genuine heartfelt injuries do not simply go away with time. We either mentally choose to forgive, or we hang on to the pain.

And we women are great at hanging on, aren't we? We replay the conversations that wounded, wincing or raging at every recalled word. We do this within the seemingly safe yet agonizingly close quarters of our minds.

Sometimes, by mysterious grace, we forgive. This, too, happens in the mind, as poisoned thoughts are inoculated by mercy. Instead of repeating hurts in our thoughts, we choose to reject the thinking that leads to bitterness. Instead of tasting the pain again and again, we taste the sweetness of healed memories.

But we cannot do this unless we live out the truths that many of us have known since childhood—the biblical truths that allow us to forgive genuinely rather than simply stick an "I forgive you (because God says I have to and it's supposed to be good for me)" Band-Aid on the wound.

Have you ever found it difficult, almost impossible, to forgive? I often find it hard to forgive because I have been deceived about what forgiveness really is. Entertaining such false notions hinders me from experiencing the gracious power of God.

The Bible uses seven different words (three Hebrew and four Greek) for what we translate "forgiveness." Fortunately for us, the occurrences of these words relating to the interaction between divine and human forgiveness are a relatively manageable (as manageable as anything in the Bible can be) number.

When used in regard to our role in forgiving others, the Greek and Hebrew verbs mean "putting aside," "disregarding," and "sending away" a debt owed to us — completely and unreservedly.[1] The word *forgiveness* also implies the relinquishment of a hateful, resentful attitude toward someone, usually someone who has wronged us grievously.

No wonder we have difficulty defining (let alone practicing) forgiveness. It's often painful, confusing, and messy. Yet because people will wound us, we must press in to what forgiveness really means in order to live at peace with others — and with ourselves.

Keeping these thoughts in mind, let's look at the toxic beliefs many women have about what it means to forgive.

~

Note: In using the pronouns *he* and *him* in the following pages, I do not mean to insinuate that men commit all offenses or more offenses than women. I wish only to keep my sentences as clear and simple as possible.

LIE 1: *Forgiveness is something I do for the people who hurt me.*
We often think of forgiveness as something we accomplish, something we're "over and done with." Personally, I wish forgiveness were like this. I wish I could "just do it." I wish I could decide to forgive, and the hurt would be gone. I am into quick fixes and solve-all answers.

We also tend to think forgiveness is primarily for the other person. Some people believe forgiveness is a way to "turn the other cheek" — to do something right to someone who did you wrong. Sometimes women see forgiveness as a way to set themselves above people who inflict wounds on them.

But these are all toxic beliefs.

TRUTH 1: *Forgiveness is a process through which I am set free.*
Forgiveness is a journey on which we embark. We enter into a dialogue with God, with our own thoughts, and with another person (or people) when we choose to forgive. We do not "accomplish" forgiveness; rather, we receive it from God so that we might pass it on to the one who injured us.

As author and theologian Lewis Smedes describes it, forgiveness is spiritual surgery on your *own* soul. He writes, "The first and sometimes only person to get the benefits of forgiving is the person who does the forgiving."[2]

In order to extend grace fully, we are neither responsible for, nor should we depend on, the reaction of the person we forgive. A person who offends us may not care that we have forgiven him. His sinful reaction, however, does not mean *we* cannot lay down the burden of bitterness.

Sadly, we cannot force someone to repent. We cannot require him to receive our forgiveness for the gift it is. A person may spit on our God-given grace the way the Roman soldiers spit on the face of Christ, who stood dying before them. Yet we can still choose to forgive for our own freedom and life.

Forgiveness is for *you*. Let the other guy face God. Let Him judge the unrepentant. No matter how the person who hurt you chooses to live, *you* can live in the joy and freedom He gives you through forgiveness. Isn't that a radical truth? Frederick Buechner expresses this truth so beautifully: "When you forgive somebody who has wronged you, you're spared the dismal corrosion of bitterness and wounded pride."[3]

As we forgive, we taste the sweetness of freedom and the hope for a future without the pain our minds have consistently replayed. The other person may never feel a whit differently than he did the moment he wounded us. But we are set free by forgiving him, and that is a divine miracle.

LIE 2: *I can't do it — some things and some people do not deserve forgiveness.*

What do you think about the terrorists who crashed planes into the Pentagon and the Twin Towers on 9/11? What thoughts flood your mind when you hear about serial killers such as Ted Bundy who brutally rape and murder women, seemingly without remorse?

Most Christians wouldn't say, flat out, that they don't deserve mercy, that what they did is unforgivable. But how many think it? To tell you the truth (I hate to put this in writing), though I probably wouldn't verbalize that the person who hurt me doesn't deserve forgiveness, I sometimes live as if I believe it.

I rationalize: *Forgiving him for this would be unfair. It would go against the principles of justice and love. Forgiving him would excuse what he did, make it seem as if what he did was tolerable, that it wasn't that bad. Well*, it was. *I demand justice.*

Has your mind ever screamed, *What he did is too awful; I can't let it go. There's no way I can forgive this; he's done this one too many times. I won't forgive; he doesn't deserve it*?

When someone wrongs us, we want two things: justice and revenge. We long for justice because He who created us is just. But we want revenge because deep down, we don't believe that justice will ever come. Sometimes we don't trust that justice will be good enough. We want people to get what's coming to them.

TRUTH 2: *Only God decides who and what deserves forgiveness.*

In forgiveness, we surrender our desires (which we see as our rights) both to judge and to get even. Forgiving sets us free from the unholy drive to settle the score and decide who gets pardoned.

But how do we let go of the toxic belief that some things and some people don't deserve forgiveness? We listen to the truth: No one *deserves* to be forgiven.

I love how Lewis Smedes articulates this: "Of course, he does not deserve to be forgiven. Nobody does. [Even] being sorry for the wrong we did does not earn us a right to be forgiven. There is no such thing as a right to be forgiven. Forgiving flows always and only from what theologians call grace — unearned, undeserved favor."[4]

We are not above the people who hurt us. We are not merely innocent bystanders. In life we wound and are wounded. When we can see ourselves as flawed, like others, we may be better able to forgive as God forgives us.

With His radical forgiveness of our sins, Jesus introduced an ethic higher than "an eye for an eye." As He cried from the cross, "Father, forgive them, for they do not know what they are doing" (Luke 23:34), Christ showed us how to forgive — mercifully, completely, and *unconditionally*.

This does not mean that we tolerate what happens to us or to those we love. We do not take the edge off their wounds or absolve them from the demands of justice. No, true and godly forgiveness is brutally honest. It recognizes the depth of the hurt and acknowledges the wrongness of it. But forgiveness does not take matters into its own hands.

What we do, instead, is let God settle the score. We allow the Judge to enforce His laws. And we trust, even when we do not see God's justice come to those who injure us, that He *always* acts justly.

Lie 3: *I forgive because I have to.*

I know this is often my attitude. Sometimes I try to scripturalize this lie by stating it in a different fashion: "I forgive because God commands me to." But it all boils down to the same poisonous mind-set: I'll do it, but only because I'm required to.

Well, yes, fine. But purely obligatory forgiveness is not true forgiveness any more than compulsory love is true love. A child forced to say "I'm sorry" might never evidence true remorse.

TRUTH 3: *I forgive truly only when I forgive willingly, as God forgives.*

Can we really forgive — even the deepest wounds? Yes, but only through a power greater than our own.

Colossians 3:13 urges us, "Be . . . quick to forgive an offense. Forgive as . . . the Master forgave you" (MSG). And how does God forgive us? Freely, because He wants to restore a relationship with us and because He loves us. Repeatedly, because He knows we fail often. Completely, because He knows that partial forgiveness is not forgiveness at all. Offering forgiveness to another under any other pretense is a charade.

In Matthew 18:35, Christ teaches that to give or receive true grace you must "forgive your brother from your heart." When we forgive, it is not because we are supposed to but because we long to be healed and want to give the other person a chance to heal as well.

Forgiving from the heart may be painful because it means reconnecting with our emotions as well as exploring corners of our minds that we might rather ignore. We forgive from the heart when we confront the lies we've believed and the bitter emotions we've harbored. By the power and grace of the Spirit, we recognize these thoughts and feelings, repent from them (these aspects of the process may take a good deal of time and effort), and ultimately receive a cleansed, renewed heart.

This regenerated, softened spirit — this gift from God — is a vessel through which Christ can pour authentic, heartfelt forgiveness. Once again, it's not easy. But isn't a heart of love, rather than a heart of bitterness, what we really crave?

LIE 4: *Forgiveness lets the other guy off the hook.*

This toxic belief brings with it a bunch of accompanying deceptions: *If I forgive, I have to forget. If I forgive, he'll be able to do it again. If I forgive, I'll have to be friends with him again.* And, perhaps most insidious, *if I forgive, I'll be weak.* Won't these things let the person who hurt me get off scot-free?

For some reason, my mind becomes a steel trap when remembering deep wounds. I can easily bring to mind some of the most painful instances in my life, even those I may have tried long and hard to forgive. Even when a person harms us unintentionally, we sometimes find it nearly impossible to forgive him, let alone trust him again. If we reestablish a friendship with someone who didn't mean to hurt us, he may never wound us again. Still we fear. Still we defend ourselves. Still we just can't forget.

I remember as a child hearing the words, "Forgive and forget." It sounded like a crock to me then, and it sounds the same now. I also remember thinking forgiveness was unfair because I believed it meant I had to invite someone back into my life (isn't that what Jesus would do?). This thought plagued me too: *If I forgive him, he'll just hurt me again.* So I would refuse to forgive. And I thought it made me strong, impenetrable, and immune to the venomous wounds of others. Have you ever been where I've been?

In the thick of unforgiveness, the only strength we can see, feel, or even conceive of is our bitterness.

TRUTH 4: *Forgiveness protects and strengthens me.*

Anger and resentment turn a corner at some point. Instead of directing their venom at the offender, bitterness and rage eventually turn inward and begin to destroy us slowly but powerfully. Unforgiveness *weakens* us rather than strengthening us.

What we often fail to realize is that we give others power over us when we choose unforgiveness. We give them power to determine the state of our emotions, to set the course for relationship with them, to hurt us again and again as we remember.

As we choose to forgive, however, we participate in a divine miracle, something that cannot be accomplished by human means. Few things are as powerful as a genuine miracle. When you forgive, you join with the Source of power Himself (see Isaiah 28:6).

Remembering an offense is easy. You hear a certain song or run into someone at the movies, and the memories of hurtful words or actions fly — unbidden — into your mind. A certain time of year or a holiday can trigger a memory so agonizing that you feel you are reliving that heartbreaking moment.

Forgiveness does not wipe clean the slate of your mind and heart. Instead, it offers you the chance to remember redemptively (see Genesis 50 for a great example of this).[5] We cannot undo the past, but we can reverse the flow of its pain. Through forgiveness, we stay truthful about what happened to us, but we choose to remember with grace. This is redemptive remembering.

Remembering redemptively is not a part of our human nature but is the work of the Holy Spirit within us. God is in the business of redemption — His "recycling grace takes our infirmities, our damaged emotions and the garbage of our lives and turns them from curses that ripple into means for growth and instruments to be used in His service"[6] (see Romans 8:18-28). Through His grace our emotions, our memory, and our thoughts are transformed. The wounds of our past become the beauty of our future.

But what if the infraction happens over and over again? What about those who injure us compulsively, regularly? Tragically, the people who wound us may very well do so again, possibly in the same way. I know this is a terribly difficult reality to accept. I hate it just as much as you do. But God addressed this problem in Matthew 18:

> *At that point Peter got up the nerve to ask, "Master, how many times do I forgive a brother or sister who hurts me? Seven?"*
> *Jesus replied, "Seven! Hardly. Try seventy times seven."*
> (*verses 21-22,* MSG)

In the verses that follow this radical statement, Christ reveals that His "seventy times seven" really means without limits (see verses 23-27). As the *Expositor's Bible Commentary* notes, "In this context, Jesus is not saying that seventy [times] seven is the upper limit. . . . Rather, he teaches that forgiveness . . . cannot possibly be limited by frequency or quantity; for, as the ensuing parable [the parable of the unforgiving servant] shows, all of [us] have been forgiven far more than [we] will ever need to forgive."[7] God forgives us — and has already forgiven us — without condition. No one will ever hurt us as much as we have pierced and will offend Christ. So, as He will enable us to do, we are to forgive despite the number of times a person wounds us.

In the equation of forgiveness, there are no numbers, only variables.

Tolerating consistent abuse, however, is *not* one of the variables. Forgiveness does not mean we invite someone to hurt us again. We can and should set limits on the amount of pain a person can inflict on us. No one would tell a spouse being physically abused to stay in the house until her husband has hit her "seventy times seven" times. Godly boundaries protect us from allowing others to injure us interminably.

And forgiving someone is not the same as inviting him back into your life, let alone back into the same kind of relationship you once had. In fact, you will never be able to restore the *precise* relationship you once had. Sin changes things (if you doubt that, read Genesis 3 for some evidence). Forgiveness makes restoration possible, but it does not make everything as good as new.

In establishing boundaries, we must keep in mind that they can be set only for the kind of relationship we will have in the future, not for how many times we forgive an offense. Smedes counsels us: "Forgiving is a gift. . . . Use the gift as often as it takes to set you free from a miserable past you cannot shake."[8]

"As often as it takes." In my mind, that is the ultimate challenge Christ issues when He declares we should forgive "seventy times seven."

~

Because of the complex nature of practicing forgiveness, I feel compelled to include the following section, which explores special circumstances that may challenge a woman's ability to extend mercy. You will find the "What Can I Do?" suggestions directly after.

What Happens If . . .
. . . the person who needs to be forgiven is me?

This often leads women to unbearable anxiety and deep depression. Many of us find it easier to forgive others for what they've done than to let go of our own sin. Have you ever felt that way? I have — many times.

The Bible does not give us explicit guidelines for forgiving ourselves. But I believe we can come up with a valid scriptural application of Truth to soothe the throbbing pain and the cries of so many women's hearts: *I just can't forgive myself. What I did was too horrible.*

Self-forgiveness is really a matter of trusting in the complete, unlimited, unconditional mercy of God. We do not forgive ourselves as much as we appropriate the perfect forgiveness that is already ours. When we finally believe that what Jesus Christ did on the cross is enough for us, we recognize that we do not need to add anything to His sacrifice at Calvary.

You do not need to beat yourself up anymore. What God did is more than enough for you. There are probably many of you who will read this and think, *Jerusha, you have no idea what I've done. It's unforgivable.* I know that you don't mean to diminish God's power when you say that; you hurt, and I grieve with you. But do you think that when God tells us that if we confess our failings, He will forgive *all* our sins and cleanse us from *all* unrighteousness (see 1 John 1:9), He really means, "I'll forgive everyone but you and everything except what you've done"?

One of the most heinous crimes I can imagine is murder. Yet David, who God calls a man after His own heart, murdered the husband of a woman he lusted after, committed adultery with, and impregnated. In Psalm 51:3, David laments,

> *I know my transgressions,*
> *and my sin is always before me.*

Many of us understand his anguish. Our sins are always before us. But as David proclaims, here is the truth that sets us free: *God forgives the guilt of sin* (see Psalm 32:5). God lovingly and freely forgave David, whose offenses included murder, deception, and infidelity. God forgives the guilt of *your* sin, too. He does not repay you for your sins.

Following our Lord's example, we must choose not to treat ourselves according to our iniquities (look again at Psalm 103:10). Forgiving yourself is really living in the truth that what Christ did on the cross is sufficient — for *you.*

And when God forgives you, He tosses your sin into the sea of His mercy. To paraphrase Corrie ten Boom's words in *Tramp for the Lord*, God then places a sign on the bank that reads, "No fishing allowed." Can we all hang up our fishing poles?

. . . I feel as though God betrayed me?

We know that God does not sin. And we also know that we need to forgive only when someone sins against us. Consequently, we never need to forgive God.

I know that this is true. I also know that God is good. I know that He is faithful. But my mind and heart often wage war on these truths. When I hurt and there is no one clearly responsible for my pain, it's hard for me not to think, *Lord, You could have prevented this.*

I know that God is not to blame for my hurt; I should trust in His providence. But I don't always *feel* the faithfulness and goodness of God. So an agonizing tension arrests my heart. Maybe you've sensed it, too. I feel that I need to forgive God, even though I know that I shouldn't and really *can't.*

Why would a Christian like me feel this way? Because it sometimes seems as if God has left me high and dry, that He has abandoned me or wounded me. These feelings may not be valid, but the pain can nonetheless be deep and lasting.

Lewis Smedes asks these penetrating questions: "Would it bother God too much if we found our peace by forgiving him for the wrongs we suffer? What if we found a way to forgive him without blaming him? A special sort of forgiving for a special sort of relationship."[9] I wonder if God, knowing that forgiveness often sets us and only us free, knowing that forgiveness is spiritual surgery on our own heart, would not mind if we forgave Him.

Of course we need to be extremely careful what we mean if we use this phrase. In Isaiah 45:9, God reminds us that He is the potter and we are the clay. He chooses what to do with us; He molds us and shapes us according to His plan. We have no right to forgive Him.

But when I say a woman might feel the need to forgive God, what I really mean is that she needs to find a place for her heartbreak, distrust, and anger. That place is an abiding, *renewed* trust in the character of God.

One of the definitions of *forgive* is "to cease to feel resentment against."[10] In forgiving God, we let go of our bitterness and begin to trust again that He is loving and kind. When we forgive God, we're really admitting that we're ready to surrender our resentment, to release our doubt in favor of peace, and to replace our anger with invigorated love. We finally concede that He did nothing wrong.

Working through this process (which, again, can take time) may actually allow us to authentically glorify God and enjoy Him *more*. In doing the often laborious task of listening to our pain, we refuse to simply stuff our sorrow under an "I shouldn't feel this way" blanket. Moreover, it enables us to trust more fully in His faithful care of us and those we love.

. . . the person didn't do it?

We sometimes find that although we can forgive a person who wounded us, we cannot bring ourselves to forgive those who failed to shield and protect us. A battered child wonders where her other parent was when beatings occurred. A sexually violated girl questions how her parent(s) could have been blind to what was happening or knowingly looked the other way.

In situations like these, the person who committed the actual offense and the person who failed to defend us *both* require forgiveness. The person who neglected us betrayed us just as deeply as (if not more so than) the one who struck the blow.

Recognizing this may help you apply to *all* offenders the truths about forgiveness that we've learned. The process will likely be difficult and complex because of the nature of your wound, but continue to take heart, consistently bringing to mind, "*Nothing* is too hard for [the Lord]" (Jeremiah 32:17, emphasis added).

. . . the person who hurt me is no longer in my life?

People who injure us and then leave us are sometimes more difficult to forgive because we have only the memory of the pain they inflicted on us. We do not have the ability to start anew, to heal our memories with a healed relationship. Whether people are simply out of touch or have passed away, not only can we not receive from them the love they denied us, but they also cannot apologize (and without a heartfelt "I'm sorry," extending forgiveness often becomes more difficult for us). In cases like this, I can only encourage you to persevere. Forgiveness is possible, though challenging. Try to focus on the truth that the person you will set free through forgiveness is yourself. Over time, you will see God — in His mercy and power — forgive through you, renewing your hope and joy.

What Can I Do?

- **Be aware of the health risks of unforgiveness.** According to the results of medical research reported in *Prevention Magazine*, people who refuse to forgive may suffer from an inability to develop healthy relationships and may have a negative attitude toward people in general, not to mention these physiological/psychological problems: anxiety, depression, poor self-image, anger, elevated heart rate and blood pressure, increased risk of heart attack, higher chance of problematic cholesterol, greater risk of blood clots, cancer, and a litany of other chronic medical issues.[11] The consequences of bitterness are real and far-reaching, possibly even life-threatening.

- **Consider your timing.** Forgiving too soon and waiting to begin forgiving each present particular problems. We may attempt to forgive quickly in an attempt to alleviate the pain of an offense. This does no justice to our spirit and is most often a false forgiveness, like a thin scab that hurriedly develops over a wound. At any time, the wound can be reopened and cause deep and unexpected agony. Remember, forgiveness is not a spontaneous act, and it is seldom a process that goes quickly. Allow forgiveness to take the time it needs. Waiting too long to start the process, on the other hand, can allow bitterness and resentment to root deeply within the heart. When unforgiveness becomes part of the fabric of our minds, forgiving becomes an even more arduous task. The only way to determine when to forgive is to ask Him who will do the forgiving through you.

- **Forgive for offenses, not for character.** We cannot forgive people for being who they are. To forgive carte blanche, we would have to be God. We can, however, extend forgiveness for specific injuries. Many times we ache because someone is not living as we know he can or as we want him to. But we cannot forgive people for being different from what we hope they would be or for being who they are. We can forgive them only for what they do. This can actually be a freeing truth if we allow it to be, for extending grace a little at a time, offense by offense, is actually possible for us, while wiping the slate clean all at once is something only God can do.

- **Forgive without manipulation.** We cannot forgive from the heart, as Christ commands us to, if we forgive with the goal of making someone realize how terrible he's been. We also cannot truly forgive if we aim to regain control of a relationship through forgiveness. Guilt-tripping someone into apologizing does not make us feel better, nor does it retain the dignity of the other person. The only way to forgive is freely, without expectation of response and without attempting to assert our power or position.

- **Recognize that the hurt may come back.** When the hurt returns, for however brief or extended a time, let it remind you of how grace enabled you to forgive once. You can forgive again. Simply because you hurt again does not mean you never forgave in the first place. On the contrary, it reinforces the fact that the offense for which you extended grace genuinely needed forgiving. Remember that God's grace freed you before. You will be able to taste the sweet joy of forgiveness again.

I refuse to hate or to harbor any form of hatred, such as resentment, ill will, jealousy—but in the moment of quick and subtle temptation, to take the matter to You in silence for Your Redemption and Guidance and Direction. . . . I am willing and eager for Thee to discipline every area of my thinking and doing and being: To wait for Your Guidance and Direction for helping others.[12]

On That Thought . . .

1. How and when have the lies we've exposed in this chapter been communicated to you (for example, from your parents, through the media, by a spouse or friend, at your church)? Through quiet meditation, invite God to heal your memory of these wounds.

2. Why do you think it's so difficult for people to appropriate God's forgiveness for themselves? Have you ever felt incapable of forgiving yourself? How might or did God meet you in that place?

3. Have you ever experienced something that challenged your ability to trust in the goodness of God? How might you approach God in order to receive healing?

4. Are there any people you can't imagine being able to forgive? Why? Have you tried to forgive them? Why do you think you have been unsuccessful? Take some time in asking God to search your heart and identify any lies that may stand in the way of receiving His forgiveness, which you can then pass on.

5. What do you think about the idea that forgiveness is first and sometimes only for you?

CHAPTER 6

ACCEPTED

Embracing Healthy Relationships

My child, if you place your peace in any creature because of your own feeling or for the sake of his company, you will be unsettled and entangled. But if you have recourse to the ever-living and abiding Truth, you will not grieve if a friend should . . . forsake you. Your love for your friend should be grounded in Me. . . . Without Me friendship has no strength and cannot endure. Love which I do not bind is neither true nor pure.

A PRAYER WRITTEN BY THOMAS À KEMPIS

Depending on which day you ask me, I might describe relationships as beautiful and complex or maddening and messy. Perhaps that is because people (myself included) are both amazingly intricate and frustratingly imperfect. In relationships with one another, our strengths and our frailties will grate or complement — sometimes both.

I discovered relatively early in life that friendships are valuable yet volatile. In elementary school, the acceptance of my classmates could set me soaring with confidence, while the pangs of rejection could send me crying from the playground.

Junior high school, a generally unstable and awkward time anyway, was full of painful experiences with gossip, boys, and trying to figure out who in the world I was. Relating to others seemed especially difficult during this time when I wanted so desperately to be liked — by everyone.

In an attempt to impress my first real crush, I tried hanging out with the Goth crowd. I took a cigarette from someone in that group and proceeded to humiliate myself after one puff by hacking for twenty minutes.

Okay, that didn't work.

So I experimented with other ways to garner the favor of my peers. I became a chameleon. With the smart crowd, I was the straight-A student. With the cheerleaders, I was the cute rah-rah girl. With my church friends, I was the eyes-closed-in-worship Christian.

I played so many roles, wore so many masks that by the time I got to high school, I had forgotten what it meant to relate to people from the center of who I was. Maybe I never knew how. Figuring that out doesn't seem to matter much. What does matter is that by the time I hit ninth grade, I feared more than anything else that people would find out who I really was (not that I knew for sure) and decide they didn't like me.

So I worked extra hard to secure myself through certain relationships. I tried to be everyone's "best girlfriend." In the meantime, relationships with guys got more interesting and gave me an even greater sense of self-assurance. If I could get a guy to flirt with me, like me, or ask me to a dance or out on a date, I felt especially significant and accepted.

How ironic it seems now, as I look back, that even receiving the attention I longed for did not sate my thirst for acceptance. It only upped the ante. The more approval I got, the more I needed. Soon I felt trapped in a vicious always-striving-yet never-getting-enough cycle.

In order to keep my friendships with girls stable and my relationships with guys thrilling, I learned to play little games. My mind worked overtime, analyzing how someone reacted to something I said, treated me on different occasions, and talked about me to others.

In college, God would not let me get away with surface, self-protective relationships any longer. As I drew near to Him, He taught me to relate to others without the mind games. It was a slow, often-painful journey.

But in my ugliest, most self-consumed moments, God began to open my ears to His still, small voice: *You are my treasured possession. I delight in you. When you are weak, I am strong. Nothing you can do will separate you from My Love. I know you on the deepest level, and I love you just as you are. You are my friend and are worth befriending.*

His words about me, and the healing process they sparked, changed the way I did friendship. As I knew more about who I was, I could relate to others more freely, more genuinely. And I can't tell you how amazing that was.

I met one of the first women with whom I had a truly intimate friendship in my second year of college. I withheld nothing from Heather. And amazingly, she still liked me. In fact, Heather seemed to care *more* about me as I vulnerably explored with her my anxieties and weaknesses.

Slowly, I allowed others inside as well. What freedom I found in my relationships as I learned to be weak in front of others. The burden of my thoughts — *Keep up the perfect front*, *Make everyone happy*, and *You are defined by who you can make like you* — was lifted, and I never want to bear that weight again.

And then God began to work on my relationships with men. I knew that the games had to stop, but I really had few tools for relating to guys, save playful bantering and coquettish teasing. I had to practice maintaining authentic friendships with men. I learned that the goal of my life was not to get the guy.

These things were not easy for me to understand or live out. Even now, the truths about relationships challenge me. My mind often threatens to spin out of control with thoughts about what my friends think about me, frailties and all.

Why, after sharing vulnerably, do I worry that I'll get the cold shoulder the next time I see a friend? Why is it that I still wonder (try as I may not to) if others will notice me? Why do I feel the need to apologize about the state of my house when friends come over? Do I believe they won't like me if I'm not a perfect housekeeper? Why is it that I still consider how I can manipulate a relationship to get what I want? Why? Because the lies I've believed (the lies many of you believe, too) are deep and pervasive.

I wage war on these thoughts because I know that healthy, authentic, godly relationships start in the mind.

Why We Play Mind Games

Before we jump into the toxic beliefs particular to relationships, I want to point you back to the fundamental lies and truths we discussed regarding our identity.

One of the foremost lies women believe about relationships is that if they have friends (or boyfriends or a husband), they will feel valuable and accepted, not lonely and worthless. On the deepest, often unarticulated level, this deception whispers, *If people love you, you must be worth loving.*

Sometimes we miss the connection between the thoughts we entertain about relationships and the bedrock truths about who we are. The wires get crossed, and instead of relating out of the confidence of beloved and treasured friends of God, we relate out of a fear that if people do not like us, we are not likable.

But friendship or romance, no matter how precious it is, will never prove your worth. When I relied on others to validate who I was, I could not genuinely love them or be fully loved by them. I was too busy trying to make sure they loved me. I pray that you will not have to fight this battle as long as I did. And I pray that as you explore your own thoughts about relationships, you will review the truths we have already discovered: You are totally loved, valued, and accepted, and who you are is not the sum of what people think about you. In the light (and freedom!) of this reality, let's look at some other lies about relationships.

LIE 1: *If I have friends, I won't have to face loneliness.*

Few things ravage a heart as much as loneliness. The dictionary uses these definitions to describe loneliness: "sadness or dejection as a result of lack of companionship or desperation," "cut off from others," "bleakness or desolation."[1]

Sounds about right, doesn't it?

Every woman faces loneliness. Whether it comes because she longs to be married and remains single year after year, because girlfriends have abandoned her or perhaps never pursued her, because she's experienced a heart-crushing breakup, because she is separated from someone she loves dearly, or because of any number of other circumstances, loneliness touches each woman and causes anguish and doubt.

No matter how many friends and dates you have, you can feel lonesome and terrified. I know because I did. I lived in constant fear that I would be "exposed" for the imperfect person I was, that my carefully constructed world of relationships would crash down around me, revealing me to be a person no one could like, no one could accept.

Many women also find that fear is a frequent companion to loneliness. We fear that we've done something to deserve loneliness, that somehow everyone else can keep friends or a man but we cannot. We fear that we will feel the barrenness and joylessness of solitude forever. Yet through the story of a Savior despised and rejected, the Bible teaches us differently.

TRUTH 1: *Loneliness is both a part of the human condition and an opportunity to know God better.*

God understands our fear and our lonesome pain. Christ Himself

> *was looked down on and passed over,*
> > *a man who suffered, who knew pain firsthand.*
> *One look at him and people turned away.*
> > *We . . . thought he was scum. (Isaiah 53:3, MSG)*

Jesus felt the scourge of others' poor opinions of Him. People looked down on Him, passed over Him. Christ knows how it hurts to be treated like worthless scum. And He felt all of this despite the fact that He had friends, even close friends in the disciples. Clearly, having strong relationships does not save humans from loneliness.

Through loneliness, however, we come to realize that only God can fill the void in our hearts for perfect companionship and love. Jesus knows that our tendency is to trust too completely in the friendship of other humans, and He allows us to feel loneliness as a means of drawing us to Him.

This does not mean that God is sadistic. He doesn't delight in our loneliness, nor does He perpetuate our feelings of isolation. Rather, He uses them to bring us closer to Him in ways nothing else could. Jesus not only understands but also heals our lonesome hearts more thoroughly than any earthly thing or person could.

The truth that God uses loneliness to woo us to Himself also does not mean that we have to feel good or put on a nice little Christian it's-okay-because-God-wills-it-and-will-work-this-for-good front when we face isolation or abandonment. Feeling alone hurts deeply. We don't have to pretend it doesn't.

Like David, we can plead,

> Turn to me and be gracious to me,
> For I am lonely and afflicted. (Psalm 25:16, NASB)

Loneliness and affliction ("persistent pain or distress"[2]) often go hand in hand, and this verse shows us where to take our agony: to God, who can turn to us and be gracious to us. Please do not dismiss as a platitude the truth that He *knows* and He *hurts* with us in lonesome moments. The Father promises, "I will not fail you or abandon you" (Joshua 1:5, NLT). Jesus assures, "I will not abandon you as orphans — I will come to you" (John 14:18, NLT). Even if you have no family, no friends, no significant other, you are not alone. He will come to you when you call. And He will never leave you, "even to the end of the age" (Matthew 28:20, NLT).

With the ever-faithful God by your side, greet loneliness as an opportunity. Listen to the pain of loneliness, for within it, I believe the Spirit can whisper things you need to hear. Bring to mind the verses of God's steadfastness often. Repeat the truth that He will not abandon you. You are not alone, even in feeling lonely. Living in that truth, you may slowly be able to see loneliness as a way to rediscover God as your all-sufficient One.

LIE 2: *The main goal of friendship is enjoyment.*

Yes, we want to have fun with our friends, but no, the primary goal of friendship is not diversion from the stresses of life. If our friendships stop there, we will be likely candidates for gossip and other forms of shallowness.

Jane Austen calls *Emma*'s Miss Bates "a great talker upon little matters."[3] It is often delightful and it definitely feels safe to speak of "little matters." We can converse endlessly of our struggles with weight or men, our frustrations in the workplace or with our kids, and the drama of our extended family without sharing anything *real* about ourselves. This is a problem.

TRUTH 2: *The true aim of friendship is fellowship.*

This may sound redundant to you, so allow me to define the word *fellowship*. Biblically, fellowship implies more than coffee dates, candle parties, or catching a movie. It is also more than a once-a-week, fill-in-the-blank Bible study. We fellowship when, in communion and partnership, we share the deepest parts of our lives.

Fellowship means obeying the command to "bear one another's burdens" (Galatians 6:2, NASB), "share each other's troubles and problems" (NLT), and "stoop down and reach out to those who are oppressed" (MSG).

We cannot fellowship only in the fun times. True fellowship requires risk. In authentic friendship we bear the burdens of others and share our own burdens — burdens such as, but certainly not limited to, anger, rejection, the loss of job and livelihood, an extended depression, even what we might be tempted to categorize as "unchristian" sins: sex and pregnancy out of wedlock, divorce, drug and alcohol abuse.

The things I just mentioned may seem like big issues to some of you. Certainly they are deep and painful struggles. And sometimes it's easier to share a big problem with other people than it is to share the daily battles of our lives — the insecurities that plague us, fears that disable us, doubts in the goodness of God, and difficulty in finding time for prayer and reflection. But these, too, are the burdens God commands us to bear for others and allow others to bear for us.

When women share each other's troubles, they are virtually unable to gossip or slander because they, too, are aching with the problem. They are sharing in the pain and wish not to exacerbate but rather alleviate the heartache.

Another aspect of fellowship is confession. David Seamands writes, "Some problems can never be solved until you confess them to others. Some people miss deep inner healing because they lack the courage to share deeply with another person."[4] The Bible instructs us, "Confess your sins to each other and pray for each other so that you may be healed" (James 5:16). Or as *Young's Literal Translation* puts it, "Be confessing to one another the trespasses, and be praying for one another, that ye may be healed." I like that because it implies that we *keep on* confessing to one another so that we might keep on living whole and healthy lives.

We are often afraid to fellowship vulnerably because it requires something of us. If we bear one another's burdens, we will feel their pain, which *hurts.* It also demands faith to confess our weaknesses to others. If we confess, we run the risk of others looking down on us or possibly rejecting us (and we've talked at length about how much we strive to avoid that!).

Though there may be risks, the rewards of pursuing authentic fellowship will be great. Women tend to stay in certain relationships because they feel secure there. But these friendships or romances may not always be the healthiest ones.

Evaluate the relationships you have now and let God guide how much time you invest in deepening present friendships or initiating new ones. Whether in making new friends or cherishing old ones, take your relationships to the next level of intimacy, and you will discover the amazing gift God gives us in fellowship.

LIE 3: *"Happily ever after" equals getting the guy.*

A particularly painful loneliness for women comes when relationships with men are unfulfilling or absent. Part of this arises from our God-given desire for companionship and intimacy, but another part comes from the lie that if you've got a guy, you've got it all.

Of all the popular paperbacks sold in the United States, 40 percent are romance novels.[5] Mary Ellen Ashcroft writes, "We invest more faith in romance than we do in God. There are stories in the early church of women longing to be free to follow Christ, of facing martyrdom in order not to be tied down by marriage. Today the chief end of a [Christian] woman is to find a man and make him happy forever."[6]

"We invest more faith in romance than we do in God." Ouch — how painfully true that has often rung in my life.

But the idea that we've accomplished something and are someone if we can get a man to turn his head or admire us is a *lie*. It's a lie that we must take "what we can get," even a man who mistreats us. It's a lie that being with someone is better than being lonely forever.

When I was twenty and feeling pretty afraid that I'd never get married (which seems funny to me now because twenty is rather young to be concerned about such things), I remember a couple of married women telling me that marriage isn't the solution to life's relational problems. In fact, they claimed, a whole host of other problems come with walking down the aisle and taking the marriage vows.

I may have nodded in interested agreement at the time, but I did not really believe what these women told me. Married women had someone to go to their work Christmas parties with. They always had a date on Valentine's Day. A lot of them had adorable kids who loved them and husbands who seemed to dote on them. *How could it be better to be single?* I wondered.

I also recall hearing the message that singleness is next to godliness. Based on Paul's statements in 1 Corinthians 7, people encouraged me to enjoy my singleness, to stay single as long as possible. The trouble was, I didn't *want* to stay single; I didn't *feel* that being single was a good (maybe even the best) option for my future.

Marriage seemed like the ultimate fairy-tale ending — the place where I could feel most fulfilled, most satisfied. And on top of it all, I sometimes heard at church that most women are "called" to marriage. It just didn't all hang together. How could being single be the godliest state when God calls most women to marriage, which, by the way, might not be all that great anyway?

We've been told and have embraced the venomous "happily ever after" deception. But what really makes a woman happy, fulfilled, and godly?

TRUTH 3: *Whether I marry or not (or whether I enjoy my marriage or not), I can glorify God and enjoy Him forever.*[7]

I remember what it felt like to wonder if I was "marriage material." Sure, I dated, but someone once told me that "dateable" girls are the ones no man wants to marry. I believed that, and I feared that I'd be alone when all my friends were building happy Christian families.

My friend and sister, we must stop thinking of marriage as the normal, most blissful state of women. Admittedly, this will mean swimming against the prevailing notions of most people and even many churches. Sermon illustrations limited to families and couples, as well as the segregation of singles to a group where — though it's not supposed to be the goal — they can meet one another and *finally* get married, do not help in this regard.

The truth is, neither singleness nor marriage guarantees either happiness or holiness. Only investing in an intimate relationship with

Christ satisfies and sanctifies us. While the untethered nature of singleness may allow a woman to serve with more freedom, being single does not automatically ensure godliness, nor does singleness always equal deep personal fulfillment. And though Christ may use marriage as a place of great joy and as a refining fire, being married does not make a woman a better Christian or a happier person. Jesus and Jesus alone brings joy, contentment, and righteousness.

Singles cannot bide their time or make their plans based on the thought, *When I get married* . . . (or, if you're trying to be super spiritual, *If God wills that I be married — but I really can't imagine that He wouldn't want me to since I really would like to*). Likewise, married women cannot assume that because marriage is difficult, they made the wrong decision. When faced with the challenges of marriage, women who have bought into the "happily ever after" lie may feel cheated and angry with themselves, their husband, even God.

Many of us, whether single or married, might have a hard time confessing it, but we've believed since we were little girls that the highest callings in a woman's life are marriage and motherhood. In actuality, the highest calling of any human — man or woman — is "to glorify God, and to enjoy Him forever."[8]

To glorify and enjoy God forever, as we are *all* called to do, women must sometimes forget. Perhaps you dated someone previously and broke up because things just weren't right. A few years later, you're still single — or unhappily married — and begin to speculate frantically, *What if he was "the one" and I missed my chance?*

We must choose to forget and leave behind the "what if" and "if only" thoughts. If we do not, the feelings will surely haunt us. One of Jane Austen's characters, Anne Elliot (of *Persuasion*), reflected on her lost love of eight years previous and explained why women don't forget: "We do not forget you, so soon as you forget us . . . [for] we live . . . quiet, confined, and our feelings prey upon us."[9]

Don't let your feelings "prey upon" you. By the grace of God, rein in your thoughts and live in the truth that His plan for you is good, even if it doesn't feel good right now. You would tell any friend of yours that very thing. It is true for *you*, too.

For those of you who are married, I encourage you to confront this lie as well. If you believed when you were single that marriage would make you happy and maybe even solve your problems, you've probably realized by now that's a false notion. As wonderful as marriage can be (and surely it is for many of us), it is nonetheless difficult and often brings a loneliness more painful than that we felt in our single years. We assume (because we've been fed this lie from an early age) that when we are with someone we love, we won't feel lonely.

As married women, we, too, need to understand that the primary focus of our thoughts and actions is not to build a Christian marriage, raise Christian children, and have a Christian home. Our minds must be trained on glorifying and enjoying God. As we do that, we free up mental space, which we definitely need to face the delights and strains that come while doing the work of godly marriage.

LIE 4: *If something is wrong in a relationship, I must have done something and am responsible for fixing it.*

I have to laugh when I think about the many times I've assumed I did something to offend a friend, only to find out later that she had felt ill, had fought with someone else minutes before seeing me, or for some other reason just wasn't in the best mood.

I really crack up when I think back to all the times I've attempted to figure out what men were thinking, especially my husband. During our first couple of years together, I probably asked Jeramy, "What's wrong?" or "What are you thinking?" at least ten times a day. Most of the time, he wasn't thinking about anything more than the song on the radio or the dinner he was eating. And when he was pondering something more, he told me.

How I wish that girlfriends of mine would be so upfront with me! Instead, we let little things erode our fellowship. The Bible, however, teaches us how to deal with broken relationships.

Truth 4: *When someone is offended, he or she should come to me; when I am offended, I should approach the one who offended me.*

Christ lays this out for us in Matthew 18:15-19 when He defines the steps for reconciliation after an offense. Do you know who He tells us should initiate? The *offended* party. Of course, there will be times when you will recognize you have truly hurt a friend and you will go to him or her, asking forgiveness and hoping to be restored to right relationship. There is no prohibition against your approaching someone you've hurt.

However, the biblical guidelines in Matthew 18 relieve us of the pressure of reading into others' actions or words. If we take people at face value, we avoid a lot of unnecessary and exhausting mental exercise. True, we may also miss someone's hints or subtle confessions of pain, but we can place our trust in the fact that God does not require us to read one another's minds. He wants us to be free of overanalyzing, self-shaming thoughts. Most often, they are nothing but pointless mental meanderings.

God (the offended party in our relationship with Him) always initiates with us, speaking through His Spirit to convict us and offer a way to reconciliation. We follow His example when we initiate with those who have offended us and also when we refuse to play the "Why doesn't he or she realize that I'm upset?" and "What in the world could be wrong with him or her?" games.

In Romans 12:18, the Lord commands us, "Do your part to live in peace with everyone, as much as possible" (NLT). There will be times when we need to work at a relationship, but there will also be times when the health of a friendship is out of our control. We learn to discern between these two as we surrender our thoughts to the Spirit, who can lead us in wisdom and truth.

What Can I Do?

- **Show people they are important and worth your time.** When we refuse to play favorites and look past a person's shoulder to see if someone closer to us (or "more important than" the person we're talking with) is approaching, we can truly listen and surrender ourselves to authentic fellowship. Jesus gave each person He encountered His full attention and His genuine concern. We should do the same. When we focus on one another, we also avoid the temptation to impress and draw attention to ourselves. You may also discover a real kindred spirit in someone you could have easily passed by.

- **Put away all gossip.** Even the thinly disguised, "I feel so bad for . . ." or "Will you pray for . . . ?" gossip. When you have been asked to keep a confidence, keep it. When you are free to share, do so with discernment. You will know if you tell another of the ache in someone else's life because you share in her pain or because it makes for an exciting conversation (or worse, because you want to hurt someone.) You will know because the Holy Spirit dwells in each Christian and convicts us of sin. Gossip, no matter how it comes out and no matter whom it's about (even your own family), is a sin. And it wreaks destruction on relationships. Proverbs 16:28 proclaims, "A troublemaker plants seeds of strife; gossip separates the best of friends" (NLT).

- **Put aside flirting and "If he would just like me . . ." games.** This point is not merely for single women. Married women still sometimes try to get the attention or admiration of men. They still sometimes think that if they could get their husbands to love them a little bit more, they'd finally feel safe, happy, and fulfilled. Whether married or single, we can *all* reject the lies that being admired by someone is better than being ignored and that "happily ever after" equals getting the love you want. We can do this by developing relationships with men that are not based on teasing, bantering coquettishly, or, more tragically, desperate attempts to secure a man's affection. I've noticed that in many single Christian circles, flirting has become an accepted and almost anticipated mode of interaction between the sexes. But consistent game playing with men sets us up for difficulties relating to men in healthy ways when and if we do marry. God can and will enable us to build holy relationships with men, relationships free of mind games, if we will only ask Him.

- **Find the people with whom you fit "just so."** I love the way Lauren Winner describes friendship in her memoir *Girl Meets God*. She writes,

> *There are a few people out there with whom you fit just so, and, amazingly, you keep fitting just so even after you have growth spurts or lose weight or stop wearing high heels. You keep fitting after you have children . . . or stop dyeing your hair or quit your job . . . and take up farming. Somehow, God is gracious enough to give us a few of those people, people you can stretch into, people who don't go away, and whom you wouldn't want to go away, even if they offered to.*[10]

We need to find these people because they will help us live out truth over the long haul. We need to find these people because they will be able to see when we've fallen into old thought patterns, often before we see it ourselves. And we need to find these people because they are lovely, fun, and a source of amazing sustenance.

- **Recognize your limits.** Today I praise God for the intimate relationships He's given me. I cherish old friends and new, and I am blessed to share my life with many. Yet I am intimate with only a few at a time. I cannot truly fellowship with a great number of people because the bearing of burdens and the building of authentic relationships take time and energy, which are precious and sparse commodities for us all.

～

Lord, make me an instrument of your peace.
Where there is hatred, let me sow love,
Where there is injury, pardon,
Where there is doubt, faith,
Where there is despair, hope,
Where there is darkness, light,
Where there is sadness, joy.
O Divine Master, grant that I may not so much
Seek to be consoled as to console,
To be understood as to understand,
To be loved as to love;
For it is in giving that we receive,
It is in pardoning that we are pardoned,
And it is in dying that we are born to eternal life.[11]

On That Thought . . .

1. What are your earliest memories of friendship like? Identify as many lies as possible that you came to believe about relationships in your formative years. Ask God for the healing balm of grace and truth to cover the painful memories this exercise may uncover.

2. Has it been more difficult for you to maintain healthy relationships with men or women? Spend some time investigating why. Review some of the lies you wrote about in response to question one. Did these lies impact the ways you related to one or both of the sexes?

3. Take five minutes to interact with or journal about the discussion of singleness and marriage in this chapter. What does it mean that a woman's highest calling is "to glorify God, and to enjoy Him forever"?

4. How do you feel about responding to loneliness as an opportunity to know God better? Do you think that is realistic or doable? Why or why not? Think of the time in your life when you experienced the most painfully deep loneliness. In retrospect, how did God reveal Himself during that time? Did you see, or do you think you could have seen, His work at the time? If you could not see Him move during that time but can see now that He did use that season for good, does that mean you did not greet loneliness as an opportunity to know God better?

5. What are some of the ways you have tried to earn people's favor? Have they worked? Why or why not? How are you tempted to secure the love of others through what you do?

CHAPTER 7

ON FIRE

Delighting in Holy Sexuality

To cope with sexuality is difficult. Yes, but everything assigned to us is a challenge; nearly everything that matters is a challenge. . . . It is not bad that we welcome [our sexuality]. What is bad is that almost all misuse and waste it. They set it out as a lure in dreary places of their lives and use it as a distraction rather than a focus on great heights.

RAINER MARIA RILKE

Over the past decade, I have watched Caitlin grow into a remarkable young woman — a woman of rich faith, zest for life, and inner beauty (all this on top of her natural physical beauty). But much of Caitlin's maturity, and even her beauty, came at a high price and through deep pain.

Caitlin and I met shortly before she turned fifteen. Vivacious, deep-thinking, and passionate for Jesus, she had the kind of charisma that cannot be learned, only given. This girl never suffered from lack of male admirers. Guys in our youth group fell for her like so many flies. But Caitlin always held men at arm's length, trying to uphold the standards she'd set for relationships.

Then she met Brady.

From Caitlin

Growing up in a loving Christian home and at a Christian church, attending a Christian school, having Christian friends, and being spoon-fed the purity stuff my whole life, I never dreamed I'd be writing these three words prior to my wedding night: I had sex.

For years I had read the books, listened to the talks, drilled it into my mind deeply and forcefully: Whatever you do, *don't* have sex before you're married. To me, that was the worst sin a Christian could commit. But when I left high school and my life started spinning out of control, I began slowly chiseling away at what I thought of as my rock-solid virtue. In the span of a few months, my parents went through a messy divorce; my mom left my father, taking my three sisters and me to live in Arkansas, where she started a whole new life; and my boyfriend of a year left me — for a man. If everyone was going to betray me like this, I figured I could give myself room for a little modification of the "Christian rules," too.

And then I met Brady — at church. That was safe, right? After all, my motto had always been, "As long as the guy is a Christian, go for it." So we started to spend time together. At the beginning of our relationship, being with Brady made all the heaviness of life seem lighter.

Though we met at church, I quickly discovered that Brady and I shared no spiritual bond. Our relationship was Christian only in name. And there was little emotional attraction — we disagreed and competed constantly. But my hurting, nineteen-year-old self, hungry for intimacy and love, *did* begin to experience an intense sexual attraction to this man. My mind felt as if it were on fire.

Brady became my "first" at a lot of things I never thought I would do before I got married. *At least it's not sex*, I rationalized. *It could be worse.* Slowly, I chiseled away at the rules.

On June 13, neither pressured nor intoxicated, I slept with Brady. I really wanted to have sex with him, so I did. Sounds simple for something that has made my life so incredibly convoluted.

I regretted it right away, but I convinced myself we were in love. I thought I would marry him. At least if I married him, we'd be each other's "only one." Things wouldn't be that bad. We would have made a mistake, but it was one that could be redeemed by our everlasting commitment.

For a while, this justification pacified my guilt. Then we started planning our days around having sex. You sort of have to stop calling something a mistake when it happens over and over again intentionally.

I loved being able to please Brady. If I fulfilled a desire of his, I felt valued. If I could offer him something he wanted, I felt needed. A relationship that I now realize should have lasted only a few months dragged on for two years. Two long, depressing, self-defeating years through which one thing kept us together — sex. This thought tethered me to Brady: I *have* to marry him; he *has* to be the only person I've been with.

Everyone else questioned my attachment to Brady. I suppose they could see it for the destructive force it was. He didn't treat me well. We fought all the time. But he was always there. The comfort and security of having someone seemed better than the loneliness of being on my own.

Brady broke up with me on January 26. I thought my life had ended. Breakdown seemed simpler than facing the reality of my sin. But somehow, through my shrieking, agonizing tears, Mercy grabbed hold of me. He whispered to me, and I begged for His help.

Hebrews 12:1 came to mind; no, it came to *life* for me. At that moment, though I can't explain it entirely, I began to throw off "the sin that so easily entangle[d]" me. I count it a miracle that I got out when I did.

I wish I could tell you that the struggle in my mind stopped then and there, but my battle raged on. Though God had enabled me to lay aside much of my sin (and the guilt of it), my mind still needed to be transformed.

As I began to grow in Christ, the reality of my sinfulness, which went beyond the mere act of sex, became painfully obvious. Thankfully, His forgiveness and grace became more incredibly real at the same time.

When Satan brings up my past (which happens frequently), God reminds me that I have been washed as white as snow, that I am fearfully and wonderfully made, that I am precious to Him. I cling to these truths, but I have to tell you that some days it's agonizingly hard.

Now twenty-four and dating the man who could very possibly be my future husband, I thank God for freeing me. My current boyfriend is hands down the most accepting person I've met. Though he knows my past, he never makes me feel dirty or guilty. But he's remained pure, and when I look at him, I fight feelings of shame like I never imagined possible.

My sin *has* been washed and cleaned; I live forgiven. Still, my mind — tainted and scarred — deals with the consequences of my actions. I've learned the hard way that it really *does* hurt when you have to tell the man you hope to marry that you've given yourself to someone else.

My relationship with Brady was really a two-year identity crisis. I temporarily validated myself with a "relationship," with sex. I lost who I was in the pursuit of what being with Brady told me I was. Now I know that no sin, not even sin that makes me feel loved and accepted for a brief time, is worth trading my identity in Christ for.

Who Deals with Lust?

Whether or not they've had sex yet, a great majority of younger women deal with feelings of guilt about sexuality — perhaps due to their experimentation with another person, their thoughts and fantasies, their self-exploration, or the things they've invited into their minds (for example, pornography, Internet chatting, and cybersex).

Some of you may have read Caitlin's story and thought, *Next to me, that girl is a saint!* Please don't dismiss this chapter because you feel the shame of your past (or present) sin beating you down. This chapter isn't merely for "good" Christian girls.

These words are for every woman who has ever thought about sex. In other words, this chapter is for every woman, single or married, sixteen or thirty-six. Regardless of where we are or have been, God has something to say to us about the war between holy sexuality and lust. Whether you feel really in control or really out of control of your sexuality, God wants you to understand your sexual nature and your call (again, no matter if you're single or married) to righteousness.

From this point on, when I refer to sex or lust, think of the particular area of sexuality with which *you* battle. Perhaps you're single and find yourself fantasizing about a colleague or a friend; maybe you're married and find yourself attracted to another man; perhaps you've been masturbating or messing around with someone else. Maybe you're married and struggle with *not* wanting to have sex with your husband. (I know some single women out there can't believe anyone would have this problem, but trust me, it's a difficulty many — even healthy and sensual — women face.) I don't know what your issue is. If you do not face sexual temptation now, thank God and pray for help if (or when) it comes!

Many people and many churches look at lust as a male issue. But Webster defines *lust* as "an intense desire, longing, or need."[1] Are we to believe women never feel intense physical desires, longings, or needs? I know I'm not the only one who, after reading this definition, would raise her hand if asked whether she experienced sexual lust.

A correlating deception is that women deal only with emotional lust. You know, because men are visual and more sexually charged than sensitive, relational women. Some people mistakenly believe that women use sex only as a means to further emotional intimacy. Others think women never really crave sex (yeah, right!).

While it may be true in many instances that women are more sensitive than men, that women tend to use sex more than men to get what they want, and that women may be less sexually aroused by sight, these are generalizations, not universal truths.

Lust isn't a guy problem; it's a human problem.[2] We want what we don't have. We long for what we cannot have yet. We yearn for what we were never meant to have. And we desire it all *intensely.*

Though we may not all struggle with lust in the same way, we all struggle nevertheless. Whether you lust to be the sexually attractive woman who steals the affections of every man who knows her, whether you lust to fulfill your sexual drives in inappropriate ways, whether you lust for a celebrity you've admired, or whether you lust for the true love who will never let you down, you have lusted. I have lusted. It's a problem.

So if lust is a human predicament, what does it tell us about our humanity? Why do we lust? What lies do we believe about our sexuality and, moreover, about our human needs and nature?

What do you think of when you read this word: *purity*?

Some of you looked at the ring on your finger or thought about your pledge to abstain from sex outside of marriage. Others may have laughed out loud. And I'll bet there are many who scowled inwardly or threw their hands up in confused despair: Perhaps everyone seems to know more about purity and why it's important (and maybe why a woman would *want* to be pure) than you do.

Let's be honest: Many of the talks we've heard and the things we've read or been told about purity have not helped us form a positive view of chastity. In her provocative book *Real Sex*, Lauren Winner keenly observes, "They seem dishonest . . . because they make [purity] sound easy. They make it sound instantly rewarding. They make it sound sweet and obvious. What's honest is this: [purity] is God's very best for us. . . . Still, many [of us] who *know about* chastity have a hard time *being* chaste. Chastity may *be* instantly rewarding, but it doesn't always *feel* instantly rewarding."[3]

Purity sometimes feels awkward, unnatural, and disappointing. The arguments we have against sex outside of marriage don't always compel us, especially when we keep on battling our desires year after year, not really understanding exactly why we are waiting.

You've probably heard the message, "Don't have sex until you're married." But is that all purity entails? I remember the first time someone shared with me that even married women need to remain pure. "What?" I wanted to scream. "I've been looking forward to sexual freedom in marriage since I hit puberty. How in the world can marriage and purity go together?"

They go together because God commands all women, married or single, to live chaste lives (see Ephesians 5:3; 1 Thessalonians 4:3; 1 Corinthians 6:13-20). A pure life is one defined by the *absence* of anything lewd or salacious, anything that contaminates or weakens a woman's pursuit of holiness. But a pure life is also marked by the *presence* of an exalted, holy view of sexuality. We don't stop needing to avoid unhealthy sexual stimulation after we're married; we don't stop needing to understand God's vision of sex once we have it. That's why the call to purity extends to both single and married women.

Christians often struggle with their sexual nature because they think God has a somewhat negative vision of sexuality. Many think the most concise way to sum up God's view of sex is, "Don't do it unless you're married." And this is supposed to convince us to practice purity? Hardly!

Linda Dillow and Lorraine Pintus beautifully illuminate God's vision for sex in their books *Gift-Wrapped by God* and *Intimate Issues*. They write, "When a [woman] sees sexual intimacy through God's eyes, she understands the holy beauty of sex. Sexual oneness . . . is a glorious picture of the spiritual oneness Christ longs to have with each believer."[4]

Sex expresses the great passion God has and has given us. To our Lord, and therefore for us, sex is not merely physical but profoundly and inseparably spiritual.

The closest earthly example we have to oneness with Jesus is the relationship between a husband and wife, who God intended to experience — but *only* with each other — the highest degree of intimacy available to mankind. Linda and Lorraine continue, "God desires that a husband and wife be naked and unashamed, glorying in the giving and receiving of exquisite pleasure and rejoicing in the intimate oneness that sex brings."[5]

Preserving or recapturing (which is *always* possible, no matter how impure a woman has previously been) her purity is what enables a married woman to abandon herself to the physical and spiritual ecstasy that Christ intended sex to bring.

What persuades us to live chaste lives is an understanding of this, God's glorious vision for sex, coupled with a commitment to obey — even when it hurts — the God who knows our desires and drives, wants us to enjoy holy sexuality, and longs to show us what sex does and does not say about who we are and how we should think.

What Does Sex Say About You?

Once upon a time, I assumed that if a guy showed me affection, he must like me. I also believed that if he cared for me enough to pursue me physically, I must be likable and attractive enough — at least for someone. If one guy thought I was worthy enough to spend time with and affection on, maybe I *was*.

Of course, then I found out that hoards of men will kiss anything that has a pulse, and I tried to laugh at my "If he touches me, I must be good enough" thinking. But I was never *really* convinced that a man's affections said nothing about my worth. I still hoped that a display of physical affection meant something more — something deep and affirming about who I am.

I know I'm not alone on this. Many women have confessed to me that they also believed if they could just get someone to touch them sensually, they'd prove — at least for a time, at least to one person — that they were worthy, attractive, and lovable. Conversely, these nagging questions often plague us: *What if no one seems attracted to or touches me? Am I not worthy of love?*

As Caitlin's story vividly reveals, the validation that sexual expression outside of marriage gives is fleeting. The acceptance and love a woman, whether single or married, may enjoy with any sex act lasts only for a moment. God never intended sexual intimacy to be a sign of your worth.

God alone knows your need to be accepted, valued, and unconditionally loved. No man can ever meet these deepest needs. No level of sexual intimacy will satisfy the most passionate cravings of your heart. And no pleasure you can give — or receive — defines or changes your identity, your purpose, or your position here and in eternity.

Keep these fundamental truths in mind as we look at some of the toxic beliefs that poison holy sexuality.

LIE 1: *Sex is the pinnacle expression of love.*

From the time I started hearing "purity" sermons, I learned that sex was beautiful and powerful and, well, the pinnacle experience of marriage. I readily admit that I may have projected some of my thoughts into the talks I heard, but I genuinely came away with the belief that sex is what a woman could really look forward to in marriage.

As a teenager, I remember asking God to let me live at least long enough to have sex. I believed sex was everything — the best thing a human could experience. And in talking with many of my friends, I discovered that they thought so, too.

Years later I got married, and my wedding night — well, the details are mine, but *wow*! And then the reality hit me that one cannot have sex all the time or even all night long. Our bodies cannot sustain perpetually intense sexual passion. Sex is not the only, or even the ultimate, pleasure of marriage — or of life.

133

I also discovered that I could not sustain continuous sexual desire for my husband. When he'd wound me, I'd want to withhold my body. Then I would feel guilty for refusing him. What happened to the life of hot sex I was promised? What was wrong with me?

TRUTH 1: *Sex is one of many amazing expressions of intimate love.*

What was fundamentally wrong was that I had built my vision of sexuality on the wrong foundation. It may have been "churchy" and even "scriptural" (in a twisted sort of way), but my thoughts about sex were not aligned with God's.

God designed sex as a divine gift that a woman gives her husband and a man gives his wife out of the overflow of Christ's love for them. Like any gift given in the right context and manner, physical intimacy reflects the love of the giver. But the Love given in sex is not only mine but also God's. Christ frees and enables me to celebrate the divine gift of sexuality rightly, as I give *His* love to Jeramy.

In *The Divine Conspiracy,* Dallas Willard describes sexual arousal and delight as an exchange of a uniquely personal intimacy with the whole person, conferred in enduring faithfulness. Willard calls sexual intimacy the mutual mingling of souls, who are taking each other into themselves at ever-increasing depths.[6] Stop with me for a moment. Let the Truth sink in. The beauty of this gift leaves me awestruck, grateful, humbled. I pray that the Lord will help us better understand sex in this way.

Sex is also a sacrifice on the part of lovers — the giving of oneself to bring joy and fulfillment to the other. It can and does make married lovers happy to delight one another sexually. But it does not *constitute* or *define* their happiness.

After our engagement, I remember joking with Jeramy (excitedly) that when we exchanged vows we'd be able to have sex as much as we thought about it. We have that freedom now, but there are times when a different expression of daily intimacy — cooking or conversing, playing with our children, or discussing a fantastic book — is better than sex. Sex is not the pinnacle experience of marriage — Love is.

Don't misunderstand me; sex is not a minor part of married life. It has an important and unique place. But it is not everything. Lauren Winner writes, "In a Christian landscape, what's important about sex is nurtured when we allow sex to be ordinary. This does not mean that sex will not be meaningful. Its meaning, instead, will partake in the variety of meanings that ordinary life offers."[7]

Sex mixes in with the sometimes humdrum but essential business aspects of marriage — things such as renewing driver's licenses at the DMV and deciding whether to replace those old blinds. Sex blends in with the love a partner expresses in making dinner when the other is too exhausted to do it. Sex mingles with the love displayed in providing for a family and navigating the difficult dynamics of relationships. Sex is one part of love, not the pinnacle or only manifestation of it.

Sex allows partners to communicate their love — born out of shared joys, sorrows, and hopes for the future — in a powerfully unique way. That's why one of the most appropriate vernacular terms for intercourse is "making love." And when spouses make love, they express levels of intimacy that go far beyond the physical. In making love, men and women declare the truth that Love, not sex, is the premiere experience of marriage.

LIE 2: *"It" doesn't affect me.*

By "it," I do not mean only sexual intercourse but also any number of things that may stimulate our senses and our thoughts — TV, movies, music, books, magazines, Internet chatting, and expressing physical affection with a man.

Every day, we're bombarded with titillating images or details of virtually meaningless sexual encounters. In our society, "hooking up" — engaging in sexual activity defined by initial physical attraction with little or no anticipation of a future relationship — has become a national sport (or a national plague, depending on how you look at it).

The world would like us to live on this adolescent, selfish, purely physical level of sexuality. How impoverished! And lest you assume this attitude is limited to unbelievers, consider these statistics revealed in studies done at Northern Kentucky University in 2003: Sixty-one percent of young adults who signed sexual-abstinence cards broke their pledges. Of the remaining 39 percent who kept their pledges, 55 percent said they'd had oral sex but did not consider oral sex to be sex. Perhaps more shockingly, a growing percentage of evangelical students report they don't consider anal intercourse to be sex.[8]

Apparently even Christian women believe that expressing their sexuality, within limits (pretty loose limits), is just fine. Oral sex? Well, within a committed relationship, what's wrong with that? Anal sex? Breast sex? (If you don't know what these are, you can be thankful.)

What is happening to us, ladies?

We also tend to see our entertainment choices as disconnected from one another: The film we watched six months ago has nothing to do with what we'll rent this weekend. The soap opera we've caught every day for six years doesn't portray lives we lust after, just ones we find . . . interesting. The fashion magazines and books we read talk about sex, but we know how to separate what we should and shouldn't dwell on.

My friend, do not be deceived.

TRUTH 2: *I am never unaffected.*

The Word of God proclaims, "There's more to sex than mere skin on skin. Sex is as much spiritual mystery as physical fact. . . . Since we want to become spiritually one with the Master, we must not pursue the kind of sex that avoids commitment and intimacy, leaving us more lonely than ever" (1 Corinthians 6:16-17, MSG). A spiritual mystery — doesn't that sound glorious? It *is* glorious.

In expressing your sexuality, you enter into a spiritual mystery, one that carries more weight than the world imagines. And you plunge into the mystery when you engage in *any* form of physical intimacy. You may enter it only in part when you hold hands or kiss. But you venture further in with each new exploration. When you caress or when you remove a piece of clothing, the spiritual mystery intensifies.

Your spirit and your body are not separate entities; everything you do with your body matters. We know when we take things too far; we can feel when we begin an emotional-spiritual, not merely physical, journey with someone. Or at least we start out being able to feel. After a while, Christian women who continually push their sexual boundaries may turn a deaf ear to the prodding of the Holy Spirit, which says, "Stop; think for a moment. I have something better for you, if you will only wait. There is a pleasure greater than this in store for you."

We can numb ourselves to the godly sorrow that leads to repentance. We can abandon the pursuit of purity, calling it impossible, archaic, or unfair. But we cannot claim ignorance any longer. You now know that your sexuality is a divine gift entrusted to you by God. You do not own this gift; it is not yours to give away — in part or in whole — whenever and to whomever you choose.

Likewise, we do not have the right to watch, read, listen, look at, or play with whatever we please. Our media intake matters. Even if we avoid graphic sex scenes or pornographic websites and steer clear of the "How hot is your sex life?" quizzes or dime-store romance novels, we are not untouched. We need to consider seriously how daily entertainment choices affect our thought lives.

In the Psalms, David declares,

> I will be careful to live an innocent life. . . .
>> I will not look at anything wicked. . . .
>> I will have nothing to do with evil. (101:2-4, NCV)

> I will set no worthless thing before my eyes. (101:3, NASB)

> I will refuse to look at
>> anything vile and vulgar. (101:3, NLT)

Are we committed to having nothing to do with evil? To setting no worthless, vile, vulgar, or wicked thing before our eyes?

Please do not misunderstand me: I am not advocating a ban on the media but rather careful reflection on what a steady diet of sexual messages does to your thought life. Does what you watch, listen to, and read encourage you to express your sexuality in holy ways?

Let me share with you how this has played out in my own life. I once read an article about single women seeking the perfect no-guilt hookup. I initially felt sorry for the women interviewed and recall thinking how glad I was that I'd never ended up in that kind of scene. I felt the same "Christian shame" for the gorgeous women I saw on TV and in movies — you know, the ones who define themselves with torrid romances and the constant pursuit of pleasure.

But despite my condescending pity, thoughts like these would creep into my mind every now and then: *I wonder what it would be like to be one of those girls. I wonder what it would be like to have sex with different men.* Or, on a particularly bad day, *I wonder what it would be like to have sex with* him. Though I confessed these thoughts, knowing they did not come from the Lord, a few months later, another article, another TV show, another film would come along and again I'd wonder.

When I got married, I didn't want to wonder anymore. I didn't want to picture myself in a relationship with anyone but my husband. But after years of attending movies that featured my favorite male stars and reading alluring "How to do it right in five minutes" headlines, I found it difficult to let go of the "wondering" habit.

A couple of years ago, I devoured three (hefty!) Christian romance novels in about four days. I wanted to put my kids to bed early just so that I could read more. I neglected laundry and dishes (something I very rarely do, thus indicating how engrossed I had become). These books captivated me.

The stories were fascinating, but they also incited lust within me — not because there was any overtly sexual content but because I longed for the thrill of the "chase," yearned for the feeling of falling in love to the point of pain, ached for the consummation of a physically tense relationship in that first, perfect kiss.

I didn't have that tension in my married life; I could kiss and be kissed. Sex with Jeramy didn't have the same mystifying allure that the idea of it did while I was single; it was fabulous, but it wasn't mysterious; it was a "sure thing." What these books sparked in me was more of the what-would-it-be-like-if thinking. And these thoughts did *not* build up my relationship with Jeramy or with Jesus.

I am not suggesting that to live lust free you should fast from the media. Your boundaries may differ from mine based on the way you are wired. I simply encourage you to look at how things impact your thoughts. Trace any actions that result from what you watch or read. Does masturbation follow the reading or viewing of a particularly romantic (or mildly pornographic) love story? Does watching a heated Hollywood affair or even a sweet first kiss cause you to go further than you intended with a boyfriend? Daydreaming and fantasy so often fuel the fire of lust.

I've also found that I connect music to past relationships. I hear these songs now, and I *remember*. Remembering is uncomfortable when one is married with children. Sometimes (how I hate to confess things like this), past boyfriends appear in my dreams. I never "do anything" with them, but even their presence reminds me of times that do not build me or anyone else up.

Though the relationship skills I learned while dating some of the men in my life certainly helped prepare me for marriage, a majority of the physical ways in which I expressed affection did not.

Perhaps you have never struggled with these kinds of thoughts or experiences. I still ask you to investigate whether your media diet proves worthwhile and edifying. The things you spend your time watching and reading may not be strictly forbidden or obviously incendiary, but do they promote *healthy* expressions of sexuality?

A continual intake of words and images that oppose holy virtues and exalt vile ones damaged my resistance to temptation and led me into danger. I don't want you to be endangered in this way. Commit with David, with me, to set no vile or worthless thing before your eyes.

LIE 3: *If my sexual expression doesn't harm anyone else, it's not that big of a problem.*

People often try to differentiate between thinking about sex and dwelling on it. This is an important, but also tricky, distinction to make.

We were created as sexual beings. God certainly could have designed another way for humans to reproduce, but He chose to bless us with sex. When I was single, I didn't always see my sexuality as a gift from God. What good was experiencing a consuming drive for something I couldn't have? I sometimes wished that God would have created my sexual instincts to kick in only after I got married.

As sexual creatures, we cannot turn off our thoughts about sex. We cannot cease feeling attracted to members of the opposite sex. How do we recognize our nature and acknowledge our drive without spiraling into lust?

There are two facets to this lie I'd like to confront. The first is a belief that if lustful thoughts don't hurt anyone else, they aren't that big of a problem. The second is an action that sometimes springs out of that logic — self-pleasuring.

Women who consistently, licentiously fantasize sometimes reason like so: "I'm not *doing* anything. Isn't thinking about sex better than actually having it?" Those who compulsively masturbate sometimes use a similar rationale: "At least I'm not hurting anyone. If I keep my sex drive to myself, that can't be such a bad thing, can it?" And those who view pornography or engage in cybersex may defend their behavior with a parallel logic: "This may not be the *best* way to deal with my desire, but I have to do *something*. At least I'm not out there doing the things I see or talk about."

Ladies, these are just more poisoned misconceptions, more venomous lies that need to be replaced with an honest admission of what is, and what is not, healthy and holy.

TRUTH 3: *When I overindulge my erotic nature in any way —
including in my own body and mind — I live a life less than what
God hopes for me.*

Because you can't get pregnant or contract an STD, thinking about
sex frequently may appear safer than actually having sex. It's not. The
spiritual, emotional, and relational dangers of lustful fantasy are far
reaching.

Masturbating compulsively, looking at porn, spending your time
playing sex games on the Internet, or any other form of sexual self-
gratification *will* compromise the health of your spirit, as well as make
it far more difficult to stop recurrent, ungodly thoughts about sex from
infiltrating your mind.

To live out this truth, let's start by looking at what is and what is
not lustful thinking. Wanting to have sex or looking forward to having
sex does not always lead to sin. Feeling aroused by an attractive man
is not necessarily lustful. Anticipating the joy of sex within marriage
is not altogether wrong. And being tempted to sin sexually does not
always mean that you have given your sex drive free reign. Often these
experiences are simply the result of being human. We have a sex drive.
We cannot always control what stimulates us. But we can choose whether
to sinfully indulge in the thoughts and sensations that confront us.

The word *lust*, derived from the Latin word *luxuria*, means to pursue
pleasure in excess. Lusting starts when we overvalue the gratification
sexual thinking or actions bring us. We lust when we overfan the flames
of sexual desire. Randy Rowland writes, "God knows that most of us
have a sexual drive that is plenty strong. It does not need to be fed."[9]

Say you have this thought: *I wonder what it would be like to have
sex on the beach* (perhaps it comes unbidden; perhaps you see or read
a scene that depicts such an encounter). You may feel spontaneously
aroused by this thought and sense your body warming, longing.

This is the moment you *choose*.

Whether or not you luxuriate in this thought is controllable.
Consciously entertaining and expanding on the thoughts that come

into your mind about attractive people, dwelling interminably on the anticipation of sex (even if it's in marriage), mentally picturing sexual encounters with a man who is not your husband — these almost always arouse lust.

But what about masturbation: Is it always a sin? When I was growing up, nobody talked about girls touching themselves; that was a guy issue (though I am now sure this was just another faulty assumption). Now female leaders of a prominent ministry report the top two issues they help single Christian women face are masturbation and Internet pornography, which includes cybersex.

I don't feel particularly equipped (or eager) to talk about this facet of sexuality. People I love and respect hold very different views on the subject. Yet I know it is vitally important that we discuss — openly and honestly — how masturbation impacts the expression of sexuality.

Within the context of this book on thought life, I am interested not so much in discussing the universal rightness or wrongness of the physical act of masturbation, but rather how thoughts that come before, with, and after masturbating can build up or tear down your commitment to holy sexuality.[10]

Some women who've never felt the urge to masturbate may try it because others talk about it. Women who've previously engaged in sexual activity may self-pleasure because they miss the arousal they once enjoyed or because they assume they cannot control their desires. Women may masturbate when they feel lonely or need to escape from the stresses of life. They may pursue sexual pleasure out of boredom, frustration, or emotional pain. If this becomes a habit, it can lead a woman into to a dangerous relationship with self-pleasuring.

And when women masturbate in conjunction with viewing images (pornographic or not) or reading materials that arouse sexual desire, this can open the door to a consuming practice. Sometimes it even ends in a compulsive addiction to an unfulfilling form of sexual expression. Lauren Winner notes, "Frequent masturbation can . . . form in us strange and false understandings of sexuality. . . . [It] teaches us that immediate gratification is a part of sex and ... removes sex from a relationship. [When] coupled with fantasizing ... masturbating plunges us into a world of unreality. .... [It can, in fact, become] a substitute for reality." And, as Winner claims, the Christian life is about living the "really real."[11] Faith is about living out the really True, the really right, the life you really crave — a life of holy pleasure.

We all know from experience that ungodly thoughts eventually leave us empty and unfulfilled. If you feel this kind of void after masturbating or if you masturbate to or because of pornography, an impure relationship, or while fantasizing, I encourage you to seek help. You may feel trapped in a Romans 7 "I do what I don't want to do" situation. You are not alone. Many Christian women have been where you are, and there is Hope.

There is also something better out there for you. Expressing sexuality in unhealthy ways is an underfunctioning of how God designed your sex drive to work. When your sexuality functions in godly ways, you experience peace, freedom, and joy.

God commands us to pursue not simply what feels good but that which builds us up in Christ Jesus. And that includes holy expressions of sexuality, which edify and protect us and the community of believers in which we live. Even sexual exploration that stays in your mind or involves only you affects you and those around you.

Lie 4: *God is keeping something good from me.*

Because I like to be gratified, this is the toxic belief by which I have been most spiritually defrauded. I like to get what I want when I want it. Waiting and me do not get along as famously as maybe we should.

I still sometimes battle this; it's another mental manifestation of the "God's holding out on me" lie that says the pleasure I can grab for myself right now is better than the pleasure I might find later (even if it comes from God.) This lie portrays the Lord as a cosmic prude who says He wants us to be happy but keeps some of the best stuff earth has to offer away from us (for what seems like forever).

Almost all humans seek pleasure. We avoid pain. These are not bad impulses, as they lead us to protect our bodies when danger presents itself and enjoy ourselves when delights come our way. The trouble comes when we become consumed with — or ruled by — any pleasure other than that found in God.

TRUTH 4: *The pleasures I can find in God outmatch everything* else.

This was a difficult truth for me to believe as a young woman. The physical pleasure that came with a great meal, an intense workout, or a passionate kiss seemed more appealing to me than the pleasure that going to church, worshipping in music, or reading the Bible could bring. To be honest, the pleasure I felt in doing "godly" things was pretty minimal.

I don't remember when things started to change on this front, but I definitely recall experiencing pleasure in God during college, which was a period of radical spiritual growth for me. By His grace (which is another way of saying "somehow, but I can't really explain it"), I realized that I had sought pleasure in the *things* of God rather than *in* God. I wish I could unpack this idea more completely for you, but it's still tough for me to attach words to the experience of God. What I can say is this: As I asked God to meet me and to let me truly know Him, things such as time in the Word or in prayer and fellowship with other believers became infused with aspects of Life and Joy I had never known.

As I read words such as "Your love is better than life" (Psalm 63:3) and "Earth has nothing I desire besides you" (Psalm 73:25), I slowly began to *feel* them. As I sang words such as "Give me one pure and holy passion" and "You satisfy me with Your love," my body *resonated* with pleasure. And as I laid aside sinful habits in which I attempted to find physical satisfaction, I recognized the gratification I really longed for was found *only* in His presence. The pleasure I began to have in relating to my Lord lessened the draw of earthly delights.

Would that I could have stayed forever in that place.

At different times, I have been enticed again to find pleasure apart from God. I have been wooed by the lies that the affection of my husband (or food or an intense run) can sate my thirst for pleasure. But again and again, God graciously reminds me,

> *"I want to show you great and marvelous things."* *(see Jeremiah 33:3)*

> *"I will never stop doing good to you."* *(see Jeremiah 32:40)*

> The LORD bestows favor and honor;
> no good thing *does he withhold*
> *from those whose walk is blameless.*
> *(Psalm 84:11, emphasis added)*

When I got married, I realized that placing sexual pleasure in the right context brought ecstasy. Having sex for the first time was a profoundly spiritual experience for me. God truly blesses the intimacy of married lovers who seek pleasure first in Him.

I feel it's important to note that if and when you marry, you may find sex initially unfulfilling. At any point in your marriage, sex may feel unsatisfying. You may not desire your husband sexually or enjoy making love the way you think you should, or at least hoped you would.

God does smile on the marriage bed, but like any other bodily experience, our sexual encounters will be laced with beauty *and* brokenness. Having sex for the first time can be somewhat akin to learning to play an instrument. Nobody picks up a violin and plays at a virtuoso level her first (or even tenth) time. From my experience, however, I can tell you that over the years, sex only gets better and better.

Does that mean there won't be struggles or seasons of dry sexual desire and drive as marriages grow? Not necessarily. Many women find their sexual drive dropping and their pleasure sometimes minimal during the exhausting days of pregnancy and raising children. Try as we may (or as *Cosmo* might attempt to convince us we can), women cannot manufacture the drive to make love or the passion that makes it rapturous. These are gifts from God and can be sought, as well as received, as such.

If you are struggling with finding pleasure in sex, have in the past, or ever do (and almost every woman will at some point), ask God to reveal or refresh your memory of the pleasure He's created for you, the pleasure He's designed you for.

Challenges with sex, one of God's most enjoyable gifts, remind us that even the pleasures God grants us on earth do not last forever. We may enjoy them — immensely — but they are ours only for a time. And the sinful pleasures we find outside of God lose their luster (notice the root of that word?) even more rapidly. They eventually disappoint and often destroy.

Only the pleasures found in God never fail, never fade. His love — He alone — is better than life. Psalm 16:11 communicates this truth so beautifully:

> You have made known to me the path of life;
>> you will fill me with joy in your presence,
>> with eternal pleasures at your right hand.

Maybe, just maybe, meditating on the fact that at His right hand are fullness of joy and pleasures evermore will renew your vision and give you a fresh glimpse of His goodness.

What Can I Do?

- **Know yourself.** Different things will trip each person's sexual radar. The older I got, the harder it seemed to kiss without wanting to go much further. I know it may sound radical, but I didn't kiss Jeramy until we were engaged. This was *not* because I was supergodly or because I didn't want to. I simply knew where I'd been and how easy it was to get there. If certain things turn you on, though this may sound simplistic, *avoid them*. Believe it or not, it's easier to steer clear of the things that trip you up than it is to turn away from them after you've indulged. If you struggle with sexual sin on the Internet, get filters (ones that actually work). If you're aroused by words, don't go into Barnes & Noble to see if there are any new books or magazines out. And though you will not be able to avoid men, you can certainly set some boundaries that will help you avoid compromising situations. The Word of God teaches us to "make no provision for the flesh, to gratify its desires" (Romans 13:14, NRSV). Without provision, your fleshly desires will wither. They will probably never disappear, but, like other fires, your sex drive can be a controlled burn.

- **View your sex drive appropriately.** A balanced view sees sexual drives as normal and healthy, challenging yet controllable. It may feel that if we don't fulfill some of our sexual urges we'll explode, but this is simply not true. Medical research shows that there is an arc that sexual arousal follows. It starts with a physical or emotional stimulant, rises, peaks, and then descends. Though sexual impulses may cause frustration and pain while they rise, our hormones will eventually return to a state of normalcy. If we exercise patience during a sexually arousing situation, we *can* control ourselves. On the other extreme, we must not deny that we have sexual instincts or sensations. Our sex drives won't disappear, even if we stuff them under Scripture and abstinence literature. Having been taught that sexual impulses could—and probably would—lead to lust, some well-intentioned singles have attempted to shut down their desires. The trouble is that if they marry, they often have a difficult time transitioning from the "no, no, no" mentality to the "I am your wife and can freely enjoy sex with you" mind-set. As with most areas of life, we must hold truth in balance. We cannot fully express our sexual urges, but we cannot deny them entirely.

- **Call sin sin.** I used to classify sexual sins as "big" and "little." Thinking a little too long about an attractive guy's body or how his hands might feel on me was a "little" sin compared to the "big" sin of actually letting him touch me like that. Reading the sex articles in fashion magazines or watching movies that made me hot were "little" sins, but doing something I read about or saw would be a really "big" sin. The trouble was, the "little" sins in my life got bigger, and all of a sudden, formerly "big" sins didn't seem all that bad. We can't let supposedly "little" sins slowly destroy us. In Song of Solomon 2:15, the Lover cries,

> Catch for [me] the foxes,
>   the little foxes
> that ruin the vineyards,
>   our vineyards that are in bloom.

Sin's destructive power has no limits. "Little" foxes (sins) ruin the beauty, the pure bloom of our vineyards. Sin is sin is sin. Christ told the adulterous woman in John 8:11, "Go now and leave your life of sin." Not just the one sin that trips you up right now — leave your *life* of sin. Now. Through His Grace, I am committed to leaving my life of sin. Amen, anyone?

- **Fight fire with fire.** The book of Job speaks forcefully: "Lust . . . is a devastating fire that destroys to hell" (Job 31:11-12, NLT). Yikes! So how do we fight this devastating fire? For starters, it's not enough to have a list of sexual dos and don'ts. Please don't misunderstand me: I am all for boundaries; I have written about sexual boundaries in four other books. We all need them. But holiness cannot be boiled down to a "manageable list of promises and prohibitions."[12] Even with the best of intentions and the shrewdest of limits we will fail unless we believe that the pleasure God can give us is better than what lust tells us we can have. John

Piper writes, "The fire of lust's pleasures must be fought with the fire of God's pleasures. . . . We must swallow up the little flicker of lust's pleasure in the conflagration of holy satisfaction."[13] Do you believe that your God is a "consuming fire" (Deuteronomy 4:24; Hebrews 12:29)? Do you *believe* that? We can fight the fire of lust only with the consuming blaze of God within us.

- **Make sure you are directing worship to the right person.** As with envy, lust is something we do *and* something we desire from others. Women lust and want to be lusted after. This desire for men's worship of us often manifests itself in the clothes we wear. When I wore certain outfits, I knew men looked at me more. For a long time, I liked how their stares made me feel. But then I began to realize that in craving the attention of men, I really wanted them to worship me. Do you follow? If they were appraising me (which would cause them to take their eyes off Jesus), their worship would be directed toward me. It knots my stomach with pity and grief when I see, on other women, the titillating fashions I used to wear. Whether they know it or not, they are often directing worship toward themselves rather than God. I don't know what's in your closet, nor will I guess why you wear what you wear. That's between you and God. All I know is that through my own experience, God has taught me to know the difference between dressing attractively and wearing clothes to get noticed or to be lusted after. No matter how nice it feels, the temporary validation that comes from an appreciative glance or comment is not worth drawing worship away from God. The Spirit knows your heart. Ask Him to reveal how wanting to be sexually desired may play a part in your life.

- **Give a godly woman permission to invade your thoughts, your habits, your relationships.** We call this accountability. And it *works.* God commands, "Make this your common practice:

Confess your sins to each other and pray for each other so that you can live together whole and healed (James 5:16, MSG). Accountability involves two people lovingly confessing, praying for, challenging, and encouraging one another to live the life God planned in the way He designed. In an accountability relationship, women exhort each another, "Have nothing to do with the fruitless deeds of darkness" (Ephesians 5:11). A good accountability partner will be able to console, counsel, and confront you. With your permission (and encouragement), she may even interrupt your dates with a "checking on you" phone call or raid your bookshelves for magazines or books that cause you to lust. Though it may feel awkward to discuss lustful thoughts or actions and masturbation or pornography, we shouldn't let uncomfortable feelings deter us from an accountability relationship. We cannot fight the devastating fire of lust alone.

- **Cling to forgiveness; release false guilt.** Discouragement associated with false guilt, which relates to a sin that has been confessed and forgiven, is one of Satan's most destructive tools. This kind of guilt incapacitates us and robs us of our joy. False guilt causes us to regret the past and fear the future, making it impossible to enjoy the present. Sexual sins tend to cling to our memories. Years after an offense we can feel dirty, shameful. Whatever sin you've committed, complete forgiveness can be yours. In Psalm 32:5, David declares,

> *Finally, I confessed all my sins to you*
> *and stopped trying to hide them.*
> *I said to myself, "I will confess my rebellion to the LORD."*
> *And you forgave me! All my guilt is gone.* (NLT)

I love the exclamation point in that translation. It expresses how I have felt so often. What? You forgive me? You forgive me! All my guilt is gone — forever. And not just *my* sin. This applies to *you*. This verse is God's Word to *you*, for *you* — forever.

⁓

*I am with you even in your tumult of self-doubt and
temptation. . . . My strength will carry you through on
wings of victory. I give you My strength. Believe I have
something better for you. . . . There is victory for every
temptation. There is victory* now. *You will not fail if
you dare to believe I have better rewards for you than
the [pleasures] you pursue outside my will. . . . In My
presence are the pleasures you crave. . . . See with holy
eyes beyond that which tempts you.*[14]

On That Thought . . .

1. How would you define holy sexuality? Which of the lies about sex are you most often tempted to believe? In what ways can you appropriate the corresponding truth into your everyday life?

2. How do the entertainment choices you currently make impact your sexuality? Are you being realistic?

3. Write down the ways in which you are currently expressing your sexuality. Don't edit. Be brutally honest (even if you are single, un-attached, and not exploring your sexuality in the ways I've described, you are nonetheless a sexual being, so I encourage you to do this exercise). Through verbal prayer or journaling, invite God into even the ugliest parts of your sexual expression. Share what God has taught you and any conviction you feel with a friend who can lovingly hold you accountable.

4. In what ways does worshipping God bring you pleasure? Have you experienced physical pleasure in worshipping God? Is it difficult for you to believe that the pleasure God can give is better than what you can get for yourself?

5. Are you directing worship to God or to yourself? Have you ever desired that a man worship you in the way I described? Invite God into those desires and memories so that you might be healed.

CHAPTER 8

SHAPED

Living as God's Masterpieces

Would that I had served my God the way I have watched my waistline!

BRENNAN MANNING[1]

I don't know exactly when I started hating my body.

I remember asking for and receiving the Get in Shape Girl exercise set for my eighth or ninth birthday. I remember feeling mortified when boys started snapping girls' bras in junior high and I had "forgotten" to wear one. I remember switching from ice cream to ice milk to nonfat frozen yogurt (no topping, thank you). And I remember thinking one day that chili cheese fries were a gift from God and the next day shunning them as evil in food form. Through all of this, however, I never imagined that I'd actually begin to despise and fear my body. I never thought I'd wage an ongoing war against the mirror and myself.

At sixth grade graduation, I won two awards. Mr. Primanti handed me a trophy for Highest Points and then gave me the Ms. Popularity certificate. But they gave Kayla — a *fourth* grader — Most Attractive Female. My insides twisted into an ugly knot as I watched admiring stares follow Kayla to receive her certificate. Though I had been told over and over again that I was cute, it apparently didn't sink in. Even at eleven, I sensed that it didn't matter how successful and popular you were if you weren't the prettiest.

From that point on, being the "Most Attractive Female" became some kind of subconscious goal for me. Back then, I never would have been able to pin down my thoughts like that. But as I grew older, I began to dwell most on the compliments I received about my appearance. It was nice if people saw me as smart or kind, but I really wanted to have everybody's vote for "Most Attractive."

In health education, I learned about eating disorders. I saw scary pictures and watched freaky movies about anorexics and bulimics. The stories didn't seem to be about people but about "-ics." I wasn't an "-ic" and was never going to be one.

Then I met people who actually *did* those things. I felt so sorry for them, never imagining that pretty soon I would be on the other side of that equation.

Like most teenage girls, I craved the attention of my female peers and found that if I talked about my body and my weight, I had an "in" with them. The girls whose approval I sought seemed interested in two things: boys and their own bodies. Happy to oblige, I conversed endlessly about how I detested my thighs or wished I could go out with whatever boy I crushed on that month.

But I still didn't hate my body; at that point, criticizing it just seemed like the thing to do. I told a friend that I had eaten only half a burrito for dinner, and she seemed impressed. I liked that. But I also remember wanting to eat the other half.

Between ninth and eleventh grades, six of my closest friends developed eating disorders. I really thought that I was immune to it, that I could help them. But all the while I was falling into the same patterns of eating little or binging like crazy, exercising to lose weight, and talking nonstop about food and my body.

Things came to a head for me in the winter of my senior year. I found out that I had been deferred from Yale, and I failed to land the lead role in our school's musical. These were the first two things that I had really wanted and didn't get. It mattered little to me that I was accepted by Yale a couple months later or that I got to be dance captain for our *Guys and Dolls* cast. In my mind, life had just spun completely out of control. Thoughts like these began to make perfect sense to me: *If I can't have everything, at least I can be thin. Thin equals beautiful. When life is out of control, at least I can decide what I will and won't eat.*

If someone would have asked me if I was going to become an anorexic, I probably would have said, "Are you kidding? There's *no way*." Anorexics weren't perfect; I saw them as needy. I could tolerate weakness in someone else, but inadequacy in myself? That needed to be worked or punished out of me — by none other than myself. No, not an anorexic; I just wanted to be *perfect.* I just wanted to be perfectly thin and attractive.

That's how it started. I really believed I could control my body, what I ate, and how I felt about it all. I really believed I could stop exercising so intensely once I got toned and that I would go back to eating normal food when I didn't have to worry or didn't care anymore. I was wrong.

I began by counting calories and fat grams. I cut back here and there but never stopped eating altogether (that's what anorexics do, right?). I exercised more, even rising before dawn to jog. I ran around our neighborhood, which had no sidewalks or streetlights, in pitch-black darkness, purging guilty calories from the day before or burning calories for the day ahead. I underestimated what I ate and overestimated how much I had to exercise in order to pay for it. And none of this seemed bizarre to me.

I believed it when I told people, "I don't have an eating disorder; I just watch what I eat. I'm really into being healthy." And I thought the way my girlfriends and I talked continuously about food and our bodies was normal. We planned elaborate low-fat meals and ate the scariest things (like fat-free butter spray — what the heck is that? — on popcorn). I dreamed about food but would wake up and steam myself broccoli, cauliflower, and carrots—for breakfast. My brother Ian will never let me live that one down.

By the time I realized I had a problem (at eighteen when I hadn't had my period in over a year), I was spending so much time thinking about my body, food, weight, and exercise that I wondered if I would ever be able to stop thinking about those things. Slowly, I began to understand that my obsession with being attractive was controlling me, not the other way around.

For the first time, I felt the *need* for a Savior. I could not overcome my controlling and obsessive behaviors on my own. I desperately needed help, hope, and healing. Jesus brought all three in abundance. He did so through His Word, through fellowship with others, and through godly counsel.

I started reading the Bible—one psalm a day. I was in college and "too busy" for anything more. Yet I quickly found that, for me, reading a psalm a day didn't satisfy my hunger for God. I began searching the Scriptures more thoroughly, and God revealed amazing verses tucked in the most unexpected places. They reflected my feelings exactly, and I felt understood, accepted.

I surrendered myself in counseling. Meeting with Dr. Vickie Harvey, I learned how my renewed spiritual passion could translate into transformed thoughts and behavior. Friends and godly mentors also supported me along the way. I asked a group to pray over my weird thoughts and behaviors in order to break the power these things had over me. For instance, I used to do lunges while I flossed my teeth in order to get a little bit more exercise in. Obviously, that is pretty abnormal. I requested and received prayer for it. Strangely, I didn't feel embarrassed by my confessions. Instead, admitting these things set me free. I also felt closer than ever to those who loved me.

Throughout my journey of healing, there were setbacks, slips, and failures. Sometimes I would fear I hadn't changed at all. But, in grace, His love would surround me once again. His vision would allow me to see the new life I'd started and would be able to continue to lead.

Whether you suffer from a clinical eating disorder, face daily disappointment with your body, or use food to assuage pain, you can experience freedom from the toxic beliefs the Adversary uses, those other people throw at you, and those your mind tenaciously clings to, all of which distract you from the truth. So let's unravel this web of deceit and pursue the peace of mind — and the peace with our bodies — that we crave.

How Do You Feel About Your Body?

Eighty to 95 percent of women report feeling dissatisfied or disgusted with their bodies.[2] Even ten years ago, the National Eating Disorders Association estimated that sixty-five million women each day were on a diet, and twenty-two million of them (that's 35 percent) would progress to pathological dieting.[3] These statistics could be significantly higher today, when Americans spend more than forty billion dollars each year on diet aids.[4] And pathological dieters don't necessarily have clinically diagnosable eating disorders. Any person who diets "abnormally" (one of Webster's definitions of *pathological*) could be included in this statistic. Abnormal dieting includes dieting as a lifestyle and obsessively excluding a food group that is part of a balanced diet, as well as using stringent programs that include only juice, soup, grapefruit, or other low-fat, low-calorie foods. Do you know anyone who has dieted or currently diets "abnormally"?

Then there are the five to ten million women — that's 5 to 10 percent of the population — who do suffer from clinical eating disorders.[5] These women binge or diet compulsively, sometimes even dying as a result of the strain overeating or starvation places on the body. But even most anorexics, commonly known as "self-starvers," do not stop eating altogether. They just eat "safe" foods and allow themselves very little, adhering to strict rules about what, when, where, and how to eat. Does this sound like anyone you know?

As many as one in five young women eat compulsively, binging on large amounts of foods; many further risk their health by remaining overweight and stagnant.[6] These women fight a psychobiological battle using food to soothe and comfort them, ignoring the body's cues to start or stop eating, and believing that food is the only pleasure and comfort they can count on.

Bulimia nervosa has been called the epidemic of our age. An *epidemic* — not a fad or trend. Up to 20 percent of high school girls and 25 percent of college-age women suffer from symptoms of bulimia. In fact, a major university resorted to posting signs in the women's bathrooms that requested, "Please stop throwing up; you're ruining our pipes."[7]

Binging and purging can become addictive because the body releases endorphins after eating, initially calming the brain and even giving it a sense of euphoria at times. This, however, is short-lived, as the bulimic then experiences guilt, shame, anger, and fear that drive her to purge the food that has been consumed.

There is another form of eating disorder, which is called, creatively, EDNOS (Eating Disorder Not Otherwise Specified). EDNOS afflicts more women than anorexia, bulimia, and binge eating disorder. These women have a constant, dangerous focus on body and weight. They diet chronically and may engage in occasional or cyclical binging, purging, or starvation.

Most women do not meet the relatively strict weight or behavior standards that would place them in the anorexic, bulimic, or binge eating disorder categories, but how many of us or our friends are just above the line, just around the edges? For this reason, some professionals include subthreshold and subclinical disorders when diagnosing women with EDNOS. According to Dr. Alan Schwitzer, "Between 25 and 40 percent of women on college campuses struggle with [hazardously] unhealthy attitudes toward eating and weight. Yet only 6 percent would be considered clinically anorexic and bulimic, indicating that a large percentage of [women] may not be getting help for [or even be aware of] their problem."[8] Sharon Hersh, licensed therapist and author of *"Mom, I Feel Fat!,"* reports, "In my practice if one out of every four [women] has a diagnosable eating disorder, two out of the other three have a subclinical disorder."[9]

Though it seems shocking to some that 5 to 10 percent of women suffer from clinically disordered eating, professionals consider this a conservative estimate. Many women are neither honest nor realistic about their own diet and exercise habits.

In our culture, preoccupation with food and weight is acceptable, even expected. In her 1998 autobiography *Wasted*, Marya Hornbacher writes,

> *Women use their obsession with weight and food as a point of connection with one another.... Instead of talking about why we use food and weight control as a means of handling emotional stress, we talk ad nauseam about the fact that we don't like our bodies.... I go to the gym, and women are standing around [complaining] about their bellies, I go to a restaurant and listen to women cheerfully conversing about their latest diet, I go to a women's clothing store and ... I have to remind myself ... [that] I don't want to look like the photos of skeletal models on the walls. Wanting to be healthy is seen as really weird.*[10]

How true I have found that to be. As hard as I try to resist the urge to criticize my body, the pressure to do so and the normalcy of doing so feels overwhelming at times. And it's heart wrenching for me to watch hundreds of the young women I work with fight a fierce mind-body battle. In part, I wrote this book because I want all of us to break free from the tyranny of the scale, the nutrition label, the diet, and the gym.

Women everywhere, at every stage of life, are silently obsessing about their bodies and their weight. We wage a battle within and are continually assaulted with accusations: "You shouldn't have eaten that. What are you doing? Do you want to be fat?" "No one will ever love you if you keep eating like that." "Your pants aren't even going to fit tomorrow."

Though we won't all develop full-blown eating disorders, many of us have distorted ways of thinking about food, our bodies, exercise, and weight. And the most agonizing part of the battle with these thoughts is usually held within, hidden from others but silently accepted by ourselves.

We've believed the lie that if we could only look a certain way or weigh a certain amount, we'd be happy, safe, fulfilled, and attractive to others. But this is a *lie*. And there are other deceptions we've believed as well. Now that we know there's a problem and understand a little what that problem looks like, let's take some time to expose the lies we've believed about our bodies and ourselves and then contrast them with the truth.

Digest the Truth; Purge the Lies

LIE 1: *If I reach X weight or X size, I'll be happy.*

This toxic belief indicates that there are "right" and "wrong" body types. And on a deep level, this lie turns into this: If I reach the perfect weight or size, I'll be loved and accepted.

For most of my life, I assumed I needed to be a particular size and shape to be beautiful. I also thought if I was beautiful, people would love me more. I know I am not alone in this. Most women with whom I've dialogued about mind-body questions confess they've also thought a certain body shape or size would make them more satisfied with life and acceptable to others — even worthy of love.

We quietly accept the thought that others base their decisions to accept or reject us largely on how we look. But why? In part, we believe it because our society has so effectively constructed a "thin myth." Carolyn Costin describes this myth well: "In today's culture, thinness represents not only attractiveness but also self-sacrifice, virtue, success, and control."[11] Our culture also sends the message that there are some "good" and some "bad" body types.

It's time to debunk this myth. A certain shape or size does not make a person more successful, valuable, acceptable, or happy. In fact, obsessing about attaining a particular body type robs us of joy and peace.

In her powerful book *Life Inside the "Thin" Cage*, Constance Rhodes details the battle in her mind regarding body and weight. She admits, "At the very moment that I was enjoying the attention I received [for losing weight], my own insecurities only seemed to loom larger. . . . My need for others to notice and approve of me [also] seemed much more pronounced during this time."[12]

I can certainly confirm this. Though I had worked hard to master my body and eating habits and though others praised me for my self-discipline and hard body, I couldn't enjoy or believe any of it. Their comments served only to reinforce the fear that if I "let myself go," I would be less likable and less desirable.

TRUTH 1: *I am a unique, beloved, and acceptable expression of God's creativity in a woman's form and shape.*
Living in this truth brings us the happiness and fulfillment we think a certain size or shape will.

Jesus promises that He "came so [you] can have real and eternal life, more and better life than [you] ever dreamed of" (John 10:10, MSG). He longs for you to experience lasting joy and fulfillment—in *Him*, not in your appearance or your body. He knows these things will never be enough; they will ultimately leave you feeling empty.

We have heard for many years that humans are as unique as snowflakes, grains of sand, leaves, or gems. Why do we distrust this when it comes to our bodies? No more! In His wisdom and inspired design, God created many shapes and sizes, body types and weights. We accept that there are people who are tall and some who are short. Some people are beautiful blondes, others have raven black tresses, and some are gorgeous brunettes and redheads. But what about the reality that some women have tiny frames, while others have bigger ones, or that some have small breasts and others have large ones? *Each* shape is beautiful because it's God's design. Why don't we believe this?

When speaking to women about this topic, I often discuss God's promise of the final resurrection when our bodies will be glorified. I ask them, "If you were resurrected in heaven with the same body you have right now, would you be satisfied?" At one time, I would have answered with a venomous, "You're joking, right?" I assumed that when we got to heaven, we'd all have model bodies. But a glorified body means perfectly reflective of the creative design of God, not a cookie-cutter, media-promoted size and shape.

Scripture tells us that our joy will be complete in heaven (see Isaiah 25:8), that we will be *entirely* satisfied in His presence (see Psalm 16:11). That means there will be no body disgust, no worrying about our waist or our thighs because no matter what shape we are, our glorified body will please our Father and will thus please us. Why should we live on earth any differently? The moment we came to know Christ, we began our eternal life and were set free from this world. You can enjoy and accept your body now, as you will in heaven.

One day as I stood before the mirror (naked, though it feels a little bizarre telling you that), I asked Jeramy, "What is a woman supposed to look like?" He seemed confused that I would ask such a question and replied simply, "You." I wish every woman could have an experience like that. A woman is supposed to look like *you*, my friend and sister. You are the precious expression of God's image in a feminine form.

The NIV translates the first part of Ephesians 2:10 as, "We are God's workmanship, created in Christ Jesus." I love this verse, but I really don't care for the word *workmanship*. It brings to my mind some kind of primitive art. In the Greek, however, the word is *poeima*, from which we get our English word *poem*. Poetry is not a crude art form; rather, it takes tremendous skill and precision to craft a poem well. And what we translate "workmanship," what I mistakenly thought of as a rough and unsophisticated artistic expression, actually means nothing less than an incomparable work of genius. As His *poeima*, you are a glorious masterpiece.

I am particularly fond of Vincent van Gogh's painting *Starry Night*. The vibrant colors, the rich textures, the subtlety and power of this masterful work simply awe me. I have come to see that God views me as a masterpiece, much like this. In fact, I love to imagine Him looking at me in the same way I view that painting — I, too, am full of passion and vibrant color, depth and complexity.

Perhaps it is not a painting but a natural work of art that makes your heart beat faster. Are you like the Rocky Mountains in God's eyes? The quiet beauty of a hidden mountain lake? Are you a sweet love song, an intricate quilt or tapestry? Imagine yourself as the most beautiful masterpiece you can. This is how God sees you. Truly.

I know there are some women reading this who are thinking, *Maybe I was* God's masterpiece as He originally designed me, but I have ruined my body by eating or dieting unhealthily and exercising too little [or for some, too much]. If I had my act together, I would be the right size, the size I could and should be.*

This, too, is part of the lie. There is no "right" size, and there is no behavior you could engage in that would *in any way* diminish your heritage as a masterpiece of beauty. Believing what God says about you actually will enable you, in the healthiest way, to take care of your body and eat with balance, freedom, and joy.

Just as the Louvre curator intently watches over and protects the *Mona Lisa*, so we are called to respect and nurture our bodies. But however we care or don't care for our bodies has nothing to do with the fact that we are — indisputably — God's priceless works of art. Whether we've neglected our bodies or surrendered ourselves to an obsession with being thin, we are still beautiful to Christ. Period.

And while He certainly desires for us to take care of our bodies — they are, after all, masterpieces — it's up to Him to express what that means. A tension will probably always exist between what we see as nurturing our bodies and what He sees as caring for His poeima. Because sin, the lies of the Enemy, and the lies of the world have so tainted our minds, and because caring for our bodies will look different based on everyone's design (for instance, diabetic women need to exercise more and eat less sugar to stay healthy), we can never make definitive, for-all-women-at-all-times statements about what eating and exercising "right" looks like. No perfect formula for healthy living exists. There is a high likelihood, however, that you will learn that caring for your body as Christ desires does not equal looking how you think or how the world says you should look.

My husband thinks a woman should look like me. And believe me, I count myself one of the luckiest women alive. So many people fight the voices of others (parents, siblings, boyfriends, or husbands) whose hurtful comments repeatedly scream in their ears, "You cow. Nobody wants a fat girl." "You better not eat that; it'll go straight to your thighs." "Why don't you go the gym today, honey? You ate quite a bit yesterday." I even remember one guy at my high school telling a friend of mine, who was *severely* anorexic, "The skinnier the girl, the better." And these lies don't come strictly from the weight-obsessed world. Far too many Christians communicate their disgust for and displeasure in the bodies of women around them.

I am so sorry and so angry for all of us who have heard these toxic messages. They are lies from the pit of hell, and every time a woman opens the fridge to binge, pushes herself beyond exhaustion by exercising, feels paralyzed by the thought of her birthday party because of all the cake that will be there, and considers herself trapped in a relationship with someone who acts as the food or fat police, I think the Enemy is laughing himself silly.

Whenever someone attacks His masterpiece, God weeps for His beloved. In Christ, we have the power to resist the lies that other people, spiritual forces, or our own hurting hearts tell us. God wants us to hear, to know, to believe, to *live out* our rightful destiny and design as His *poeima*. He aches to woo us back to His heart and to show us His exalted vision of the body and food.

When the lie comes that you are not the "right" shape or size, argue back (even if it means saying it straight to your biggest critic's face), "I am the expression of God's image. A woman is supposed to look like *me*, God's masterpiece."

Will you stop with me and soak in this truth? Will you ponder it this week for as many hours as you've been assaulted by the toxic beliefs you see on TV and billboards and hear from body-loathing men and women? Spend an equal (if not more) amount of time immersed in the truth that you are lovable, acceptable, and declared worthy of happiness and fulfillment. We will recapture the joy we can have in taking care of our bodies and adorning them beautifully only when we trust that doing so does not add to our worth but merely reflects it.

In no way would I advocate abandoning the care for and enjoyment of a healthy body. But it's time to finally disregard the lie that we will be happy, accepted, and lovable when we reach the "right" weight. The question of our happiness, acceptability, and lovability was settled forever on Calvary. You are approved of and lovable. Your body type is beautiful.

LIE 2: *What I eat or don't eat doesn't matter to God.*
I have consistently succumbed to this powerfully toxic belief. In my mind, the dissatisfaction I felt with my body—and the eating habits that resulted—was just about my body, nothing more. I did not think that what I ate or didn't eat impacted my relationship with God or, by extension, my relationships with others.

But the food we consume—and why we consume it—is tremendously important to God because we so often eat or don't eat based on lies we've believed.

TRUTH 2: *Eating is not merely physical but also spiritual.*
Following Christ is a very fleshy, messy business. The perfect expression of His love was a broken *body*, and He commands us to remember Him over a sacred meal. He is the Bread of Life and Living Water.

The Bible also indicates that sharing a meal is neither a hedonistic pleasure nor, at the opposite end of the spectrum, a joyless "eating to survive" practicality. Biblically, breaking bread implies fellowship in the deepest sense. To share a meal with others is to invite them to experience and celebrate Life with you!

And this does not mean that in order to experience the spiritual dimensions of eating, we always have to dine with another person. In reality, we *never* eat alone. Every day, we break bread in the presence of our beloved and omnipresent Jesus.

Whether or not we actively acknowledge it (or show appropriate gratitude for it), eating displays our dependence on the Creator and Sustainer of life and also commemorates His body and blood, broken and spilled out for us. How tragic that we often trade this exalted view of eating for a distorted, worldly one.[13]

One of the most devastating effects of our war with body image is diminished spiritual joy and development. As we obsess about our weight and size, spend more time in the gym than we do with our Lord, compete and compare with other women, and squander our resources by purchasing excessive diet or exercise aids, we steal from our spirit, our relationships, and, ultimately, from God.

In Romans 14:20, Paul urges, "Do not tear down the work of God for the sake of food" (NASB). Together, let's refuse to destroy the work of God for the sake of food or for the sake of a body type or weight. Instead, let's reclaim the sacredness of eating.

LIE 3: *If I can control my body and my weight, the rest of my life won't feel so out of control.*

I have tried controlling my body as a way of controlling my life. Have you ever done this by eating—or by not eating? I also believed I could decide when to start and stop engaging in weird eating patterns and depending on exercise to "earn" food or assuage "guilty eating."

Other women have believed they could insulate themselves from the world with a thick layer of flesh and weight. Some think if they become large enough, no one will bother with them anymore. Ironically, this behavior is simply another way women try to rule and protect their own lives.

Author Marya Hornbacher, who chronicles her struggle with body image in *Wasted: A Memoir of Anorexia and Bulimia*, tells her audience about the experience she once had flipping through a book on disordered eating and body image. The book talked extensively about the medical consequences of overdieting. She claims that reading about those consequences didn't faze her. But she confesses that the secret that book didn't reveal was if it didn't kill you right away, fixating on your body could control you the rest of your life, slowly destroying you. She wishes she would have known that. You and I have been given the knowledge she didn't have. Now we must choose.

You may feel that you have control right now, but please believe me when I reemphasize that control is only an illusion. As you are drawn deeper and deeper into the obsession with manipulating your body and weight, you will discover that your obsession already is, or is on the way to, controlling you. This illusion of control is tragically devastating. While I thought I was in control, my infatuation with food, shape, and weight had actually enslaved me. And the more I clung to the deluded thought that I could gain control "if only I . . . ," the more defeated and powerless I felt.

TRUTH 3: *God is in control of all things, including food and my body.*

As we've discussed in previous chapters, we often try to control our lives because being out of control feels scary. We fear that if we lose control of our bodies, disaster will follow. If we choose not to eat, it's often because we assume that if we control how much food we put in our bodies, we won't have to worry about our weight — or our problems.

Even if you don't diet, develop an eating disorder, or surrender yourself to overeating, you may live in a state of continual discouragement regarding your weight and appearance. You can become controlled by obsession with your body whether or not you lose or gain weight. Remember, it's your *thoughts* that count most. Preoccupation with your body will control and, in the end, kill your spirit. It may even take your life.

We cannot control our bodies any more than we can control anything else (remember the other sections on control?). We can do certain things to help maintain a healthy body — eat wisely, exercise appropriately, and so on — but even these cannot guarantee we'll have a body shape or size we like. God alone can and does control all things.

Lie 4: *Unless I have an eating disorder, I don't have to worry.*
Another aspect of this lie is this: If Christians aren't supposed to obsess over their bodies, I guess it doesn't matter how I eat. Häagen Dasz every night? No problem! McDonald's three or four times a week? What's wrong with that?

I am not an expert on the right way to eat. In fact, my husband would tell you that I have pretty weird tastes (for instance, my two favorite things to eat for breakfast are cheesecake and pizza — but not together!). I spent so many years eating sparsely that I sometimes swing to the opposite extreme and eat rather unhealthily, claiming French fries and ice cream as my "right." I also sometimes eat junk food for comfort or out of frustration (ironically, when I feel disgusted with myself, I sometimes turn to food to make me feel better).

Now, there is nothing — I repeat, *nothing* — wrong with eating fries or ice cream (especially Starbucks Mud Pie ice cream). And there are times we all eat for emotional or social reasons — we may not be hungry but still take a piece of cake at a friend's birthday party just to join in the celebration.

But should we do this every day? Does eating like this all the time show care for God's masterpiece? Should we consistently eat non-nutritious foods or plan our meals based on our emotional state? Does the fact that I have recovered from an eating disorder mean I'm out of the woods when it comes to the health risks associated with unhealthy eating?

Often, at least for me, it does not. I know that I tend to struggle more with negative thoughts about my weight and shape when I do not give my body the nutrients it needs to stay physically and emotionally balanced. I may not like to eat foods high in protein as much as I do bagels, but I need to balance my wants with my body's needs.

TRUTH 4: *My body pays the price for poor habits.*
The truth is, physical and emotional devastation can happen to those who engage in any unhealthy eating patterns. Over the last few years, a surge of news reports, articles, and even movies have addressed the fact that eating too much (especially certain kinds of nonnutritious foods) and exercising too little put women at risk for serious health concerns. The idea that eating fast food every day does not encourage weight balance is pretty much a given. But did you know that there are also emotional side effects such as mood swings and irritability that come from neglecting the care of our bodies?

Yo-yo dieting, occasional binges and purges, excessive exercising, and periods of excessive or limited food intake (or even moderately indulgent or restricted eating over long periods of time) can result in health problems that people typically associate only with clinical eating disorders. These may include the following symptoms:

- Headaches

- Dizziness

- Insomnia

- Heart palpitations

- Shortness of breath

- Irregular menstrual cycles

- Change in skin color and tone

- Persistent halitosis (bad breath)

- Frequent or chronic fatigue

- Stomach cramps

- Constant hunger

- Tooth enamel loss

- Irritability

- Mood swings

- Loss of sexual interest

- Yeast infections

- Bowel problems

- Osteoporosis (early onset)

- Body aches[14]

Let me unpack a couple of these health concerns and show you how they can impact the average dieter. First, consider the problem of mood swings. Discouragement with one's body can manifest itself in a pessimistic, disappointed attitude, while body "success" can result in a temporary high. Guilty, dejected thoughts can literally produce chemical changes, which may eventually lead to clinical depression.

And what about irritability? In *Temptations Women Face*, Mary Ellen Ashcroft asks, "How many of us have snapped at our [family members] or been irritable with a friend because we were feeling guilty and condemned about eating two brownies or because our dieting stomachs ached for food?"[15]

And let's look at another bundle of concerns: the excessive acid produced in the stomachs of those who diet frequently (stressing their bodies through lack of food or through the consumption of non-nourishing foods) as well as those who frequently binge (which causes the body to produce digestive acids in larger amounts). Disproportionate stomach acid causes bad breath, stomach cramping, and even tooth enamel loss.

Consistently eating more than one needs may stretch the stomach, making it difficult for a person to recognize the signals of hunger and fullness. A heavier body can also lead to problems such as acid reflux, irritable bowel syndrome, and stress on the heart.

Even superhealthy eating programs can become compulsive. There's actually a name for this, coined by Dr. Steven Bratman: orthorexia. "Orthorexics obsess over what to eat, how much to eat, how to prepare food 'properly,' and where to obtain 'pure' and 'proper' foods." They sometimes "feel superior to others who eat 'improper food,' which might include non-organic or junk foods."[16] Constance Rhodes rightly notes, "Again, at issue here is the loss of balance. By placing such a heightened importance on every ingredient [or the nutritional value] of the food that is eaten, the orthorexic is no better off than the anorexic, bulimic, or binge eater when it comes to the hold that food and eating have on their lives"[17] — and on their minds.

We harm our minds and bodies by believing that as long as we don't have an eating disorder, we're okay. We need to care for our bodies, recognizing that our thoughts about weight and food do affect our health.

What Can I Do?

- **Stop verbally criticizing your body — period.** What? No more "I feel fat"? No more "I saw that milkshake land right on my hips"? Nope. I'll tell you why: The less you verbalize these things, the less you dwell on them and the less power they have over you. We don't know exactly how this works, but while the Enemy and his minions do not have complete access to our thoughts, they still seem to tempt us in the areas of greatest weakness. Do you think it's possible that when we verbalize things such as "I hate my thighs" or "This makes me look fat," the Adversary picks up little ways to attack our hearts and minds? Let me repeat: The less you verbalize these things, the less you will dwell on them and the less power they will have over you. Don't believe me? Try it. Stop saying, "I feel fat" for two weeks and see what happens. There's another benefit attached to this decision not to criticize your body as well: You help other women overcome their issues when you refuse to be part of the "I hate my body" club. You help them find other things to discuss and discover the delight of relationships free of subconscious competition and comparison.

- **"Talk back" to your thoughts.** When we've heard negative thoughts enough times, we stop challenging and simply accept them, assuming they are part of the normal fabric of our minds and lives. Instead, we need to fight thoughts with words. We need to replace the toxic phrases that used to define our thoughts (*I feel fat*; *I hate my body*) and replace them with more powerful, positive, and *true* ones. I think it's even best to speak the thoughts out loud. Let me walk you through what talking back might look like.

  - **Thought:** *I ate too many pieces of bread at that Italian restaurant last night. I'd better not try to put on my jeans (even though I wore them the day before yesterday). I'll wear my "safe" pants.*

  - **Response:** "I refuse to be afraid of a pair of pants; instead, I claim my God-given freedom and beauty. The gauge of my value is not in whether my jeans fit or not. Even if I did eat too much, that doesn't have to determine my mood."

Now, if you try on your jeans and they feel uncomfortably snug, you certainly are not obliged to wear them. Who wants to wear too-tight pants? You *are*, however, called to set aside any fear that might come with the fit of your clothes. Remember, it's your *thoughts* that count, not whether you force yourself to wear something that makes you physically uncomfortable.

If you are a habitual overeater, use this opportunity to confront the feelings and thoughts that led you to overindulge. If you are (or have been) preoccupied with being thin, ask yourself, *Does eating too much bread on one occasion matter in the grand scheme of things?* Despite what you may think, the answer is no. What *does* matter is choosing *now*, wherever you have been before or will be tomorrow, to live, think — and eat — in Truth (see Matthew 15:17-20).

- **Enjoy your *whole* body.** In other words, stop focusing on those areas of your body that you dislike. My stomach has always been the body part I liked least. In fact, I used to touch my middle every few minutes to make sure it had not magically expanded (my neurosis revealed once again!). I can laugh about that habit now, but I still sometimes battle thoughts about my stomach. I now have lightning-shaped stretch marks and will never have a "six-pack." But there are things I *can* enjoy about my stomach. It is responsive to the soft touch of my husband. It has a cute little belly button in its center. It works really well (even in pregnancy I never had reflux or digestive problems). I am blessed with my stomach. When I focus on disliking my stomach, however, I then begin to view my thighs and my complexion in a more critical light. I feel less satisfied with my hair and my overall tone. See what I'm getting at? For many of you, it will be a different part of your body. Maybe you hate your bust size or your legs. Whatever it is, can we stop fixating and start enjoying? Try complimenting your body, your *whole* body, for the beautiful masterpiece it is. And enjoy revealing the beauty God has given you. You show off, in a way *no one else* can, a unique aspect of God's glorious image. Deep down, don't you want to do that? In their book

Captivating, John and Stasi Eldredge claim that on a fundamental level, all women want to unveil beauty:

> *Beauty beckons us. Beauty invites us. . . . God—beauty himself—invites us to know him. . . . He delights in alluring us and in revealing himself to those who wholeheartedly seek him. . . . A woman does too. She fears it [often because she may not be found beautiful "enough"], but below the fear is a longing to be known, to be seen as beautiful and enjoyed.*[18]

God is stunning. He lavishes beauty on the world. His beauty resides in *you* and in every woman, for all have been created in His enthralling image. As you begin to enjoy your whole body, you will also begin to unveil your transcendent beauty.

- **Put an end to competition and comparison.** When a woman walks into a room, do you size her up? When you walk into a room, do you place yourself in the standings of attractiveness and fitness? Do you watch how slender women eat and try to match their habits? Do you feel ashamed when you don't or superior when you do? How many agonizing times I have battled these kinds of thoughts! But how good it feels when I refuse to go there in my mind. We must make an active choice not to hold ourselves up against friends, family, or even strangers. God's Word speaks about women clearly: "When they measure themselves by one another, and compare themselves with one another, they are without understanding" (2 Corinthians 10:12, RSV). When we measure ourselves by other women, comparing ourselves to them and competing with them, we evidence that we do not understand our individual, indisputable worth in Christ. I am and *you* are a one-of-a-kind masterpiece!

- **Consistently evaluate cultural messages.** Ads, movies, music, and television all communicate their own version of reality. But most of these are false realities. There is no can of diet soda that will make guys follow you around like lost puppy dogs. There are no workout tools that will slim and shape you to a "perfect" size (especially since no such thing exists). These cultural messages are damaging and lead to destructive thought patterns. Refuse to allow cultural messages to penetrate your mind and show up later, masquerading as your own thoughts.

- **Get the help you need.** We all need to seek God's help in discerning the real doubts and fears behind our thoughts. We need to surround ourselves with women who have made a commitment to live in freedom from the tyranny of body and weight pressure. We need the support of friends and family who can help us sift through our thoughts. We all need prayer and wisdom. But if you are struggling with food, body, or exercise and cannot seem to break free of the patterns, seek additional help. I mentioned earlier that after I recognized that my obsession with body and weight was out of control, I needed to see a counselor for some time. You may need to see a medical doctor as well. Most of all, we need to spend time with God, receiving the healing He longs to give to His hurting ones.

⌒

O blessed Lord, you ministered to all who came to you:
Look with compassion upon me, who through unhealthy
relationships with the body have lost so much of my
health and freedom. Restore to me the assurance of your
unfailing mercy; remove from me the fears that beset
me; strengthen me in the work that will renew my mind

*and transform my thoughts. In the Name of the Father,
the Son, and the Holy Spirit, Amen.*[19]

On That Thought . . .

1. What are the first thoughts you remember having about your body? Have people in your life made hurtful, disparaging comments about your body? How did these early experiences shape your past and present body image? How might inviting Jesus into these memories change you?

2. What is the most frequent thought you have about your body right now? Invite God into your thoughts and dialogue with Him about the lies and truths highlighted in this chapter.

3. Write down the part of your body you like the least. Explore in a journal-entry manner when you started noticing this dislike and whether there were any experiences or comments from another person that began or confirmed your concern. How can you begin to enjoy that very part of you? If you're discussing this question with a friend or a group, focus on the truths about enjoying our bodies and revealing our God-given beauty. We all know how easy it would be to end up on a this-is-what-I-hate-about-my-body tangent. And despite what we may be used to, I hope we know this is not where we want to go with our friends or even in our own minds.

4. Are your friends concerned about their bodies? Do you talk about it frequently, even if in lighthearted or joking ways? Are you ready to stop criticizing your body and participating in body-loathing talk? Tell God and invite Him to respond.

5. How might Jesus describe your body? Would it be difficult to see yourself with His eyes of passionate love and grace? Spend some time asking God to reveal how you might do so. Listen.

CHAPTER 9

OVERWHELMED

Allowing Sorrow to Draw Us Near

*Lord, I am desperate. It comes down to this: Are You real?
Please help me; don't refuse to answer me, for if You are
silent, I might as well give up and die.*

FROM MY JOURNAL

"Every day for a year, I begged God to let me die."

This is how a friend described her depression to me. I grieved with her over that time riddled with pain. Having faced depression myself, I empathized with the depth of her struggle. We talked about how difficult it was to face depression as Christian women, how we often felt confused by or ashamed of our experiences. We both wondered, *I'm supposed to be filled with hope and peace; how can I be depressed?*

Many Christian women have settled for a life of decreased vitality and joy. They don't recognize themselves as being depressed, or they don't want to acknowledge their depression. Some think, *There's nothing terrible in my life. I haven't been abused or had to deal with a death or divorce. I shouldn't be depressed.*

I wish these women could meet my godmother, Stephanie. She radiates; she glows with Christ's love. Stephanie calls everyone "sweetheart"

179

and "dear" and *means* it. She regularly speaks at women's conferences. Her life and faith have touched thousands.

And Stephanie has faced deep, persistent depression. Come with me as she shares her story.

A Cork Bobbing to the Top

I don't remember a time when depression *didn't* play a role in my life, though I didn't recognize my condition as depression for many years. My major symptoms — lack of motivation, a general sense of unrest and sadness, fear of failure and disappointment, chronic procrastination — could have been issues anyone faced.

No single experience triggered my depression. I hadn't been neglected or abused. My parents raised me in loving faith. They taught me to trust in Jesus from an early age. I married a wonderful Christian man. My career looked promising. Nothing seemed particularly wrong with my life.

When I worked full-time, my schedule didn't allow for much reflection. I had deadlines to meet and people to please. Busyness kept some of my depression at bay, but not all of it. Some days in the late afternoon, I would look at the clock and think, *Stephanie, you've wasted another day*. Phone calls unreturned, letters unanswered, projects incomplete — they all taunted my mind with vicious words: *You might as well just give up. Did you really think you could do anything of value?* I would lie in bed at night and think, *Wasted, wasted, wasted*. I questioned whether life was worth living. I entertained the thought that it might not be.

When work became sparser and I had time on my hands, the days and nights of feeling dejected became more frequent. Close friends and loved ones knew of my battle and encouraged me to see a doctor. "These feelings don't go away no matter how much you do or how much you pray," they pointed out.

Somewhat reluctantly, I made an appointment with a psychopharmacologist, a doctor who specializes in the study and prescription of drugs that affect the mind and behavior. I answered his questions honestly and explained the vague yet persistent sense of gloominess I felt. I then informed him that I would be glad to do anything he asked me to do, *except* start taking Prozac.

You must understand that this all happened twenty years ago when Prozac first hit the market. The stigma attached to it and a fear of the unknown made me adamantly resistant to taking such a drug.

"Guess what," the doctor told me. "I think you may be a good candidate for Prozac."

This was not going according to my plan.

"I'll make you a deal," he said. "I'll run a serotonin screen [a test some doctors use to determine a person's likelihood of serotonin deficiency], and we'll see if it indicates you'd benefit from Prozac. If the results come back positive, you try it. If they're negative, we'll look at other options."

I agreed. The technicians ran and read the tests. Apparently I needed Prozac.

One month later, I returned to report on the efficacy of my "depression drug." I told the doctor exactly how I felt — like a cork bobbing to the top; like a woman who understood "normal" for the first time.

Speaking to depressed women across the country — at churches and seminars, in retreat halls and sometimes even in the ladies' room — I've been able to see that God uses all kinds of things to treat depression. Medication is not a complete solution for depression, though it helps some of us in the battle. Deciding to take medication if a doctor prescribes it for you is between you and God. There are no universally right or wrong answers in regard to the questions about antidepressants. The key is always that a woman seeks God first and combats the toxic beliefs that have led or contributed to her depression.

After years of battling depression, I am finally able — by the grace of God — to see that even when I think I have wasted a day, the Sovereign and merciful Lord has better equipped me to love Him. For He has given me another minute, another hour, another day to talk with Him, to draw near to Him.

He's also shown me that in my moments of greatest weakness, He can still use me. I remember slapping on "my face" (aka makeup and a smile) and rushing out the door to give a lecture to a couple hundred women even though all I felt inside was emptiness.

I used to beat myself up with words like *hypocrite* and *fake*. But I now know that when I speak Truth, even when it's difficult for me to believe, Christ receives the glory. His truth is truth whether I feel it or not.

When the feelings of worthlessness, hopelessness, and despair come and when thoughts threaten to overwhelm me, I thank God that He's given me Himself, as well as medication, to fight the lies and live in Truth.

I might have subsisted at a level of diminished joy and fulfillment for my entire life. Or I might have experienced such deep depression that I took my own life. It could have happened to me. The thought *I don't have a reason to be depressed* could have indefinitely prevented me from seeking treatment.

Instead, God allowed me — like a cork — to float to the top, to breathe freely, to see His hand lifting me up. You cannot put a price on that.

The Mind-Body Dilemma

Depression affects everyone. If you've never been depressed yourself, you probably know one or more people who have faced major depression (defined by two or more weeks of seriously depressive symptoms) or chronic, low-grade depression (feelings of sadness or hopelessness that may not be life debilitating or cause a woman to become nonfunctioning but still erode the peace and joy of a woman's mind).

The National Institute of Mental Health reports that one in five women experiences a major depression during her lifetime. NIMH findings also indicate that women are twice as likely as men to battle depression.[1] Yet more than two-thirds of people suffering from depression never seek treatment.[2] Many women live with symptoms of depression, believing that their harassed emotional state is normal or is a result of their own faulty living.

Some people, even some churches, think depressed women will — or should — eventually "get over it." But telling a depressed woman to suck it up and get back to living only reinforces the ache inside her heart that cries, *Something is wrong with me. Did I cause this? What if this never goes away?*

Depressed women "may be moving on the outside, but inside they are slipping deep into the quicksand of alienation and isolation."[3] They often feel pressed down, weakened, sunken. "Inactivity [or overactivity], as well as difficulty in thinking and concentration"[4] frequently accompanies depression. Sufferers often feel a relentless, palpable sense of futility and worthlessness.

Yet depression is not strictly an emotional condition. It affects the entire body by infecting the brain. Both the thought processes and the physical functioning of a depressed woman are impacted. Common physical symptoms include interruption in sleep, appetite, and sexual cycles. A depressed woman's immune system is compromised, and she may experience muscular or nerve pain. And none of these conditions are created or imagined.

Jesse Dillinger, a Christian counselor, likens depression to a prolonged LSD trip. I know that sounds crazy, but trust me, her comparison is outstanding. LSD is a psychotropic drug. It literally changes the way a person thinks by causing the brain's neurotransmitters to malfunction.

Synapses misfire. And when a woman's brain ceases to function properly, her ability to think clearly is impaired.[5]

Depression does pretty much the same thing — it causes disturbances in brain functioning, which completely changes a woman's ability to think normally. Since I have been clinically depressed, I guess I can relate to people who have acid trips.

Depression is both a physiological and a cognitive condition. Consequently, it must be addressed physically, mentally, and spiritually. Some doctors write prescriptions for every patient suffering from depression, disregarding other factors that contribute to a person's well-being. Some counselors downplay the importance of medication, insisting that therapy (or prayer) will solve depression. But research shows that most people suffering from depression respond best to a combination of psychological, spiritual, and physical treatments.

A depressed person's body must be carefully treated if he or she is to experience peace of mind and soul. Attention to diet, sleep, and the general nurturing of the body aids in the healing process. Medication may also help.

To combat my first postpartum depression (maybe a story for another book), I took Prozac, and the depression began to lift as soon as the drug got into my system. But the medication did not solve all my problems or erase my fears. This is why we cannot focus solely on physical factors, neglecting the emotional and spiritual dimensions of depression.

Depression impacts the thoughts we entertain, the ideas we confront, the state of our souls. Depression usually challenges a woman's sense of worth and confidence. Depression almost always undermines a woman's ability to experience pleasure in daily life, even in activities she previously enjoyed. And depression can lead to serious doubts about faith and God.

Feelings like these, whether instigated by a physiological condition or a psychological one, should not be ignored. These dark places of the soul can be explored with the help of godly counsel. A depressed person will probably find help from either a professional or lay counselor — maybe both.

As a woman looks at the emotional and spiritual aspects of depression, she will be changed. The deep-seated joy of being set free from negative thought patterns may also trigger physical reactions that relieve biological symptoms. Depression may even draw a person closer to the Lord. I would not trade for anything — even a life without depressed feelings — the intimacy with Jesus I discovered in battling depression.

There is no perfect way to treat depression, no one-size-fits-all approach to healing. But there is one Truth — Jesus Himself — who speaks into the joyless void of depression. Let's look now at some toxic beliefs about depression and the truths that conquer them.

Allow me to preface this section with a word to those of you who are currently battling depression. I now know from personal experience that until some of your depression lifts, it may be difficult to distinguish between lies and Truth. During my own depression, I could barely read a sentence (even in the Bible) without feeling condemned. Everything spoke hopelessness and futility to me.

If you are there today, my heart is with you. My mind has faced the same assault. I have believed that God's Word could not apply to me.

As far as you are able, let God's truth simply wash over your mind. Wherever you are right now — even in the valley of the shadow of death — Christ walks with you. I know because He walked with me.

Will you journey with me, as you are able, into the freedom of Truth?

What Does Depression Say to You?

Lie 1: *Even God can't love me.*

Of all the distorted thoughts that depressed or formerly depressed women have shared with me, this is the most consistent.

Depressed women often feel distant from God and wonder how He could love them. Many believe that they have done something to offend God and that He has afflicted them with depression because they deserve it. Some women carry the weight of past sin around with them, sure that God can't love them. They may have asked for His forgiveness a thousand times, but they've never felt the assurance of His love.

In the darkest days of my depression, I thought God was punishing me for my selfishness, that He was angry with me for my pride and greed and the ways I had mistreated others. My picture of God included a scolding expression and wagging finger, if not a rod ready to strike me and "bring me back into line." But that is not how God saw me — or how He sees you.

TRUTH 1: *God loves me. God values me. God accepts me.*
I just don't know how else to say it, though I fear you might skip over those commonly heard words.

Instead, I pray that Truth would sink down into your heart with fullness of life. I pray that the grace and beauty of His love would pierce you as never before. "God loves you" is not a platitude or a simple answer for all of life's hurts. It is the most radical, most complex truth of your existence, the most poignant hope of your heart.

God's love does not change or falter like our love does. He loves you no matter what you've done or will do. He loves you without condition, without regret. He loved you no less when you did that terrible thing, when you entertained that wicked thought. He loved you then with the same redeeming, relentless love He loves you with right now — and *forever*.

Even the sum of your worst transgressions cannot come close to extinguishing the consuming fire of God's love. Psalm 103:10 tells us,

He has not punished us as our sins should be punished.
He has not repaid us for the evil we have done. (NCV)

During my depression, I thought God was punishing me. And I could usually find some sin I could link this perceived punishment to. But if we take God at His Word, we can trust that He does not punish us according to our sins. Furthermore, what He says about your worth, your acceptability, and His love for you *never* changes. Hebrews 13:8 proclaims, "Jesus Christ is the same yesterday and today and forever." That means God, who *is* Love, looks on and treats you with the same love yesterday, today, and *forever*.

LIE 2: *I am alone.*

Depression and feelings of isolation, abandonment, and alienation go hand in hand.

Depression can be caused by many things. Many women resent the fact that life has not turned out the way they hoped or planned. They grieve the death of a cherished friend or family member. They feel undervalued by everyone, abandoned, and alone. Some depressed women have, indeed, been neglected or abandoned. They have been excluded by peers and alienated from former loved ones. They don't believe anyone understands their pain, even God. Many women feel angry with God but unable to express their conflicted emotions. Their disappointment or anger often surfaces instead as depression.

Most depressed people withdraw from family and friends, even from activities that require them to interact with people. This reinforces feelings of loneliness and estrangement. In moments of deep despair, we doubt anyone's been as deep in the pit as we are. But Scripture paints a different picture.

TRUTH 2: *I am* not *alone.*

When I felt abandoned and, for lack of a better word, crazy during my depression, I found strength and courage by looking at the examples of great men and women of God who faced feelings of devastating sorrow. Depression doesn't discriminate; it has affected even the most faithful Christ-followers:

- Hannah, "in bitterness of soul. . . wept much (1 Samuel 1:10) and "would not eat" (verse 7). She kept "praying . . . out of . . . great anguish and grief" (verse 16).

- The prophet Jeremiah wailed, "I am the man who has seen affliction. . . . [I] walk in darkness rather than light" (Lamentations 3:1-2).

- Elijah prayed, "I have had enough, LORD. . . . Take my life" (1 Kings 19:4).

- Solomon lamented, "I hated life. . . . All of it is meaningless, a chasing after the wind" (Ecclesiastes 2:17).

During seasons of depression, I either wept until bitter tears seemed all I knew or else I could not cry at all. My heart, numb but somehow still throbbing with pain, felt so heavy that I could not move. Food tasted like ash in my mouth; I refused even my favorites dishes. How could I eat when all I could taste was pain? The world seemed shrouded in darkness, and a fog of exhaustion descended on me. I wanted to die. And when I read the Bible, I felt condemned and afraid. Every verse I read seemed to scream, *You're not good enough. Stop pretending. God can't love a weak, helpless woman like you.*

Lies! Wicked, hateful lies.

God tenderly met Hannah and fulfilled her longing. Jeremiah felt the presence of the Lord more intimately in his grief than in any other time. God sent an angel to sustain Elijah. He used Solomon to rule Israel and write many of the proverbs. Jesus met me, too. And He meets you in your pain. He is there now — lean in; listen.

God *loves* broken, hurting, depressed people. He *uses* broken, hurting, depressed people. Their wounds become the source of hope and life for others. Where would we be without Samuel, the son born because of Hannah's grieving prayers? How would we know that His mercies are new every morning (see Lamentations 3:23) if Jeremiah had not walked through darkness into this enlightened truth? Would Solomon have seen the power of God's wisdom so clearly if he had not discovered that all human striving is meaningless?

And, perhaps most significantly, God *understands* depressed people. He knows how you have felt, how you feel. You are not alone. Hebrews 4:15 teaches, "We don't have a priest who is out of touch with our reality. He's been through weakness and testing, experienced it all" (MSG). Christ shared fully in all of our experience, including the feelings of deep despair that mark depression. Jesus Himself was "a man of sorrows, and familiar with suffering" (Isaiah 53:3). Matthew 26:37-38 records these words of Jesus: "My soul is crushed with grief to the point of death" (NLT).

You are *not* alone. Depression told me that nobody understood me, that I would be alone forever, that there was no hope for me. God provided me with the promises that when I am brokenhearted, He is close to me (see Psalm 34:18) and that "weeping may remain for a night, but rejoicing comes in the morning" (Psalm 30:5).

Jesus understands. Even when you think death would be better than life, He understands. He knows how it feels to be alienated, isolated, and abandoned by everyone — even God (see Matthew 27:45-46). In those moments of deepest loneliness, let His nail-scarred hands clutch you.

LIE 3: *Things will never get better.*

Another emotion that can rarely be separated from depression is hopelessness. To a depressed woman, the possibility that the heaviness weighing on her will lift seems remote. For a Christian woman experiencing depression, the hopelessness may be compounded by this confusing paradox: If a believer is the residence of Hope (the person of the Holy Spirit), can hopelessness overcome her?

Tragically, it sometimes does. I remember feeling so strongly that nothing would ever change, that nothing would ever get better. I feared that my life would amount to nothing, and I had no hope for the present, let alone for the future.

I feared waking up because I would have to face another meaningless day. I feared lying down because I would be tormented by hopeless thoughts. Like Stephanie, and like many of you who will read these words, hopelessness robbed me of energy, joy, confidence, and peace. I couldn't see how even if my circumstances changed, my heart could ever be restored. I felt crippled, sapped, drained.

In the bleakest hours of my depression, I seriously considered suicide. In fact, at one time, I thought God wanted me to take my life. Now I can't even imagine how that idea seemed reasonable to me. It's almost as if that were another person altogether.

Please believe me: I understand how much it hurts to feel that nothing will ever change. I know how it feels to be so depressed that you don't think life is worth sticking around for. Only one Truth can lift us out of this pit.

Truth 3: *God will not let me go; in the end, I* will *have joy.*

If I have something to hope for, time seems to pass more quickly and my attitude tends to stay more positive. Even when I'm hurting, the hope that my pain will eventually end keeps me plodding along.

The pain I endured delivering my daughter Jasmine was intense. She came so quickly (within two hours of my arrival at the hospital) that the nurses did not have time to give me any medication — not even ibuprofen. Since I had what is called "back labor," it felt as though someone were driving a stake into my spine.

What made matters worse was that Jeramy, my husband, coach, and Jasmine's daddy, was a hundred miles away (praise God, he drove like the wind and dashed into the delivery room a few moments prior to her birth).

Before he showed up, I remember virtually clawing my way to the bathroom and telling Jesus, "I can't do this. I feel so alone; I think it would be better to die than face this pain." There have been few times I've heard his voice so clearly: "I am here. I will uphold you and deliver you."

These two thoughts sustained me: Jesus promised to be with me, and my baby will be here soon. This pain feels unbearable, but a greater joy — a new life — will be mine very soon.

In a similar way, God comforted me in my depression. He promised He would not let me go. He assured me that hope would be, and already was, mine — now and forever. He showed me His deliverance, even though it took longer than I would have hoped.

God promises that a joy greater than every human suffering will be ours, a joy more complete and consuming than we can even imagine. We can endure depression only in light of this glorious hope.

Perhaps we have heard these verses from Revelation 21 so often that their radical significance eludes us: In heaven "God himself will be with [us]. . . . He will wipe every tear from [our] eyes. There will be no more death or mourning or crying or pain" (verses 3-4). Do you believe that this life awaits you? Do you believe that this hope impacts your life *now*?

It often felt too difficult for me to imagine heaven's Hope in my present life, yet I have begun to see that truly, truly (as Jesus might say to us), "our present sufferings are not worth comparing with the glory that will be revealed in us. . . . Creation itself will be liberated from its bondage to decay and brought into the glorious freedom of the children of God. . . . We . . . groan inwardly as we wait eagerly for . . . the redemption of our bodies. . . . [And] in *this hope* we were saved" (Romans 8:18,21,23-24, emphasis added).

With all creation, the depressed woman waits for liberation from the bondage to decay. She groans inwardly, anticipating the redemption of her body, the freedom from a broken mind. In this hope she was saved and continues to grow in her salvation.

This is your hope: A greater joy, a glory that far outweighs your present, past, or future sufferings awaits you. A full liberation, a complete redemption, an eternal salvation is yours.

And this hope is yours *now*.

It's not enough for me to say, "I'm sorry you're hurting. But all you have to do is look at things in the light of eternity." While this may be true, when you're depressed, you need something to cling to *now*. What we can clutch is the edge of His cloak, just as the woman did who bled for twelve years but had faith that "If I just touch his clothes, I will be healed" (Mark 5:28). (Read Mark 5:24-34 for more details of her hope when all hope seemed lost and of Christ's all-powerful mercy, which immediately freed her from suffering.) When we hurt in the here and now, we can remember that Christ understands and that He can and will heal.

Few of us see instantaneous results or know healing within a few days. For many of us, seasons of depression stretch on and on. Like the afflicted woman, we may need to do something — perhaps touching Christ's robes today would include one or a combination of the following: prayer, spiritual direction, medical counsel, and medication. Like Jesus, we may need to wait, even while walking through the valley of the shadow of death, for God to deliver us. Each woman's experience will be different.

No matter how desperate we are, God does not fear our circumstances, our doubt, or our hopelessness. He is familiar with *all* our ways, and He understands the battle we face. He does not merely give us hope; He is our Hope — a hope far greater than we can conceive of. That hope is mine, and it is yours. That hope is your eternal inheritance and your promise for today.

His purpose for us is life — true and lasting life. He died to purchase for us "real and eternal life, more and better life than [we] ever dreamed of" (John 10:10, MSG).

Do you believe that a greater hope awaits you? Do you believe there is something more for you — right now — than this mortal world? Faith, hope, and love cry out, "Yes!" Will you echo those cries with me? Will you proclaim with me that this life is worth living in light of His faithfulness?

LIE 4: *Depression is a sin.*

Unfortunately, people who don't understand depression have wrongly projected, "Depressed people just need to read their Bible more, pray more, stop focusing on themselves, and get right with God. They must be living in sin. God is probably punishing them for something they've done."

How I wish I could erase these toxic lies from the consciousness of every depressed person! When depressed, I heard these accusing statements in my own mind. I certainly didn't need anyone else (or the church) to reinforce such ideas.

False notions like these have wounded others, too. Someone actually attempted to exorcise one of my friends during her battle with depression. She recounted this incident to me as one of the most horrific and humiliating experiences of her life. My friend did not need exorcism; she needed mercy, grace, and love.

During my depression, I endeavored to "fix" myself by becoming a better Christian. I tried to have "long enough" quiet times, claim the promises of the Bible, and fix my attention only on Jesus and on the needs of others. I racked my brain, searching for unconfessed sin that might be plaguing me and isolating me from God. And, as I told you before, I assumed that He must be punishing me for something. Why else would I hurt this badly?

Then the doctor who delivered Jocelyn (my oldest daughter) suggested that I might want to try Prozac. I felt even more helpless, powerless, inadequate, and dejected. To me, taking medication was the ultimate sign that I was too weak to handle my own life. They gave antidepressants to people who couldn't deal, right? I genuinely believed that taking medicine meant that I was weak and that I wasn't a good enough Christian. Was my depression a sin? Was taking medication for a mental condition a sin? If not, why would some people say so?

TRUTH 4A: *Depression is not a sin.*

People often treat depressed women as if something is wrong with them. Well, guess what, something is wrong with *everyone*, and it's not always the result of his or her own sin. Depression is part of our fallen humanity. It comes with the territory.

The wrongness of our bodies simply comes as a result of the Fall. Because fallenness weaves its nasty threads through the fabric of all creation, every single woman lives in a broken, needy body with a broken, needy mind. Depression is no more sin than grief or cancer — also results of the Fall — are sins.

And, try as we may to make it so, neither sanctification of the mind nor glorification of the body are instant processes. Conversion does not free us from the fundamental human condition — weakness of body and spirit.

God never tells depressed people to "get it together" and act like good Christians. He woos them into His presence, where compassion and mercy flow, where love heals. He understands. He does not send the hurting away with the commands, "Get into the Word more. Pray more. Have more faith. Just get over yourself." Instead, His tender voice promises,

> "A bruised reed [I] will not break,
> and a smoldering wick [I] will not snuff out." (Isaiah 42:3)

When you are bruised and breaking, when the fire of your faith smolders, He doesn't condemn you. He doesn't withhold healing until you become a "better Christian." He looks at you in the company of the many holy saints who have battled as you battle.

But what about medication? Is using antidepressants against God's will? If I had lived fifty years ago, before the introduction of psychotropic drugs, I might have taken my life. If I had not done that, I probably would have suffered from severe depression for a long time (at least the first few years after delivering Jocelyn).

I thank God for medicine that has allowed me to experience more of the real, lasting, and full life that Christ redeemed me for. Taking antidepressants or other forms of depression medication does not equal weakness any more than using insulin to treat diabetes does.

Even if I have to take medicine for the rest of my life, I will praise God that it's available. I will rejoice in the brokenness of my body because it allows me to see that He provides for my every need. Jesus wants you to experience the abundant life that is beyond what you can imagine. And if He wants to use medication to help you experience that life, please don't turn Him down because you believe taking medicine is a sign of spiritual weakness. Thank Him with me that we don't have to struggle on our own but that we have doctors whom He's allowed to develop these helps.

Again, this does not mean that every depressed woman needs to or should take antidepressants. Some women will not even respond to psychotropic drugs if they begin taking them. Great discernment (and sometimes a bit of trial and error) is required to find the balance between attending to all the aspects of depression—biochemical, psychological, and spiritual.

Perhaps "depression is a sin" seems like such a foundational lie that you wonder why I did not place it at the beginning of this chapter. Allow me to explain: Depression — the physiological response to imbalance in the brain — is *not* a sin. However, we must look at two additional facets of the truth to fully understand the validity of this statement.

TRUTH 4B: *Sin can contribute to depression.*

Had I opened the chapter with this truth, some women may have stopped reading immediately. At one time, I would have. I would have assumed that everything I believed about myself was, in fact, accurate. "Well, thank you, where is the nearest gun?" might have been my attitude.

In a healthier place now, I understand that sin can contribute to depression. Sin sometimes even results in depression. Look with me at the example of David in the book of Psalms. Fleeing for his life from a jealous, infuriated Saul, David felt the weight of despair, exhaustion, and spiritual isolation. He experienced what we would identify as depression when he moaned, "Why, O LORD, do you . . . hide yourself in times of trouble?" (10:1). "My bones suffer mortal agony as my foes taunt me . . . all day long" (42:10).

The bodily and emotional turmoil David endured during this time was not sin nor a result of sin. Yet we see in David's psalms 32, 38, and 51

195

how sin can contribute to, and even cause, depression of the body and soul. In 38:3-8, David cries,

> *My bones have no soundness* because of my sin.
> *My guilt has overwhelmed me*
> *like a burden too heavy to bear.*
>
> *My wounds fester and are loathsome*
> because of my sinful folly.
> *I am bowed down and brought very low;*
> *all day long I go about mourning. . . .*
> *There is no health in my body.*
> *I am feeble and utterly crushed;*
> *I groan in anguish of heart. (emphasis added)*

If you ask me, David sounds depressed. And he does not keep the reason for his depression a secret: "Because of my sinful folly . . . I groan in anguish of heart." David's sin brought on a depression that became physical.

David's sin (adultery) may seem like a "biggie" to you. But depression does not come solely as the result of "really wicked" sins. My own sins of worry, self-absorption, control mongering and manipulation, anger toward myself and others, focusing on the urgent and neglecting the eternal — these things have contributed to and sometimes led to depression in my own life.

C. S. Lewis claimed that God often uses diseases of the body to cure sicknesses of the soul. Amen. I believe God may have allowed depression at some points in my life to help heal the brokenness of my heart and mind.

When dealing with postpartum depression, it was difficult for me to accept that I was, all at once, physiologically depressed due to a hormonal imbalance (that I could not control) *and* spiritually depressed because of my sin, which became more evident during this time. When I could control virtually nothing and often felt too weak to try, my control-freakishness (I say that in the most loving way possible) came into sharp focus. And when I had no idea how my body would end up looking as it recovered from pregnancy, my self-focus, my obsession with body image, and my concern over what others thought about me also became overwhelmingly evident.

The essential thing for each woman who faces depression to do is humbly go before the Lord and pray that the cause of her despair would be revealed. Through medical treatment and counseling, I walked through the biological and spiritual elements of my depression. And that was hard. But praise God, on the other side, I can see that depression can be related to sin, can be caused by sin, and may actually be both at the same time.

TRUTH 4C: *Depression can lead to sin.*

Because depression distorts our thinking, we often become more vulnerable to temptations of the mind during seasons of despair. We may worry seemingly uncontrollably. We may find it nearly impossible to forgive. We almost always doubt the truth of God when depressed, in large part because our brains are not functioning properly. In moments like these, the grace of God meets us and lifts us to a place we cannot get to on our own. He does not condemn us but uses helps such as counseling, prayer, medication, and His Word to nourish and sustain us until we can think more clearly.

During times when sin has led to depression, however, a woman may be tempted to think, *Well, I've already blown it; I may as well keep on sinning.* For example, a woman who indulges in sex before marriage may face the guilt of her sin and become depressed. Instead of repenting, she may respond with a "since I can't become a virgin again, it doesn't matter anymore" attitude. In this case, depression leads to more sin.

Anger, resentment, and bitterness make many women depressed, but rather than confessing their sin or forgiving, they hold on to their rage and their unforgiveness, believing that if they let go, they'll have nothing left to hold on to. This, too, is sin.

Depression can lead to sin, just as *any* set of emotions can. Every feeling prompts us to make one of two choices: glorify God or serve self. A depressed woman may have a difficult time discerning the way of escape from temptation that God provides for her (see 1 Corinthians 10:13). Her physically depressed condition may make her vulnerable to sinful enticement. However, she and loved ones can anticipate and pray over this.

Remember, depression is *not* a sin. But remember as well that sin may lead to depression, and depression may lead to sin. Keep these things in mind and *in balance* as you look at your own experiences with depression, as well as those of others.

What Can I Do?

- **Get the help — and *keep* getting the help — you need.** Many Christian women mask their depression or attempt to spiritualize it away instead of getting help. Maybe they don't want to seem weak. Maybe they don't really believe they have a problem. Maybe they fear they're crazy and nothing will help. Maybe they just can't bring themselves to do *anything*, let alone call a therapist or doctor, make an appointment, and keep it. If you have lived or are living with depression, please get help. And remember, getting diagnosed with depression does not equal getting help. A diagnosis is the beginning. Depressed people need to *keep* getting help. Years later, I still need to see a doctor to make sure my brain stays balanced. I have seen three different therapists over the course of my life. The process of recovery from depression may last a long time. But if you get the help and keep getting the help you need, you will not only experience freedom in your present grief but also have resources you can turn to when future troubles come your way.

- **Set modest goals during seasons of depression.** At the worst points in my depression, I could barely do anything at all. I had trouble doing simple tasks, even getting out of bed. A friend helped me at the time by advising that, with reliance on the Spirit's guidance, I choose three things to do each day. Though it was difficult for this perfectionist woman to face, even if God told me that two of my goals should be to shower and get dressed that day, I had to trust that I should obey. If you are depressed, don't try to snap out of it by throwing yourself into life's duties. Maybe it sounds crazy or weak to have to ask God what to do before you get out of bed. All I know is that it made my day more bearable to think, *I just have to do the three things He wants me to do. I can make it through those things.*

- **Remember.** Neither time nor renewed joy has erased the memories of my suffering. Stephanie has not buried the ache of her days of darkness. Jeremiah writes,

I remember my affliction and my wandering,
      the bitterness and the gall.
I well remember them. (Lamentations 3:19-20)

We cannot forget depression, nor should we, though anyone who has dealt with it would probably like to. By revisiting the darkness in our memories, however, we

call [this] to mind
      and therefore . . . have hope:
Because of the LORD's great love, we [were not and never will be]
      consumed . . .
      his compassions never fail. (verses 21-22)

Remembering my depression helps me to consider again the amazing faithfulness of God. Recalling the bitterness of agony brings closer to my mind the sweetness of His deliverance and compassion. Don't "get over" your depression and leave it in the past. Let the mercy of Christ flood your memory, showing His glorious grace in sharp contrast. Remember so that even if He needs to walk with you through the valley of the shadow of death once again, you will recall and will not be consumed.

- **Comfort others with the comfort you have been given.** Depressed people are all around you. And they need Christ's healing balm. They need His light, hope, peace, and love. But they sometimes cannot find it on their own. Like the paralytic carried to Jesus by his friends, we sometimes cannot come to the Healer by ourselves (see Luke 5:17-26). Second Corinthians 1:3-5 exclaims, "Praise be to the God and Father of our Lord Jesus Christ, the Father of compassion and the God of all comfort, who comforts us in all our troubles, so that we can comfort those in any trouble with the comfort we ourselves have received from God." Sometimes we receive comfort. Other times we can give comfort. May the comfort God gives you in suffering flow over into the lives of others.

O Father of mercies and God of all comfort, our only help in time of need: I humbly beseech thee to behold, visit and relieve Your sick servant. . . . Look upon me with the eyes of thy mercy; comfort me with a sense of thy goodness; preserve me from the temptations of the enemy; and give me patience under affliction. In thy good time, restore me to health, and enable me to lead . . . my life to thy glory . . . through Jesus Christ our Lord. Amen.[6]

On That Thought . . .

1. List the lies you have believed about depression. Which of these lies has impacted your view of depressed people (including yourself, if you have experienced depression) most powerfully? Why?

2. What do you think about the idea of taking medication for depression or for other psychobiological conditions, such as schizophrenia or panic disorder? Why do you think you have this attitude? If you found yourself struggling with severe depression, would it be easy or difficult for you to accept a prescription for psychotropic drugs?

3. What is your view on counseling? Is counseling different from therapy? If you discovered that your insurance would not pay for a Christian counselor, what would you do? Why?

4. What role does sin have in depression? Do you agree with the statement "Depression is not a sin"? Why or why not? How would you help a friend who is both physically depressed because of a chemical imbalance and spiritually depressed because of prolonged exposure to negative thinking?

CHAPTER 10

In Time

Focusing on What Really Matters

Did it ever occur to you that the root of all your trouble
was that you had not life enough? It is so.

GEORGE MACDONALD

Everyone adores Andrea. Fun-loving, deeply spiritual, and a great listener, Andrea draws others to herself quickly. If you ask people to describe Andrea, they use words such as *spunky, passionate, devoted, compassionate, merciful, tender, fun,* and *real* (people seem to use that word with emphasis). Some of the young women Andrea has mentored have even chosen the word *hero* to describe her.

Like I said, everyone adores Andrea. That makes it all the more tragic that in the past, Andrea struggled fiercely to validate herself with a long list of Christian activities. Though most people fell in love with Andrea's empathetic and warm heart almost instantly, she thought doing "good" things was necessary to earn and secure their love — and God's.

Bondage to people pleasing and what she saw as Christian "duty" ultimately left her sapped and apathetic. It took what she calls a two-year purging of her soul for Andrea to realize that she couldn't keep up the feverish pace at which she was living. And, more important, God wasn't asking or expecting her to do everything.

Andrea's breakdown/breakthrough started right around her twentieth birthday. Here's how she described it to me.

From Andrea

For the first three years of college, I lived for relationships. In fact, while at the university, I focused far more on people than I did on academics. Looking back, I realize that most of my friends were people I was trying to help. I spent hours and hours listening to their problems, trying to encourage them and help them live in the freedom and joy of God. I felt tired, but I assumed I was doing what He wanted me to do.

My parents served as missionaries/pastors to international students, and I watched them minister all my life. I definitely didn't realize it back then, but both my mom and dad struggled to maintain healthy boundaries with their time. It seemed natural to "lose yourself" in doing God's work. And isn't that what believers are supposed to do anyway — "lose themselves"? Aren't we supposed to work tirelessly, bringing others to Christ and helping them grow in Him?

Discipline had always been one of my strong points, and I applied that to my faith with vigor. Structured prayer and devotional times were part of my daily ritual. Missing a day made me feel lazy and disobedient. I served faithfully (and frantically), leading Bible studies and singing with the worship band.

But during the summer after my junior year of college, I shut down. It didn't happen all at once, but by October of my senior year, I had basically ceased doing anything other than going to class, doing homework, and occasionally pretending to be happy when I was around my close friends and family. And when I didn't "have" to do something, I became lethargic, felt apathetic, and struggled with laziness.

I couldn't imagine doing anything that would bring me joy. But I feared silence and solitude more than I can express. What would I hear in the silence? Would I have to face myself if I sat quietly for five minutes? Noise became my constant companion: I listened to music and watched TV and old movies. Basically I kept my life loud enough to drown out my own thoughts and what God might be trying to say to me.

Though I knew I couldn't get away with ditching church, I stopped praying, stopped reading the Bible, stopped ministering. I just stopped. And I simply couldn't pull myself out of the funk of fatigue and indifference.

Finally, I knew I had to get help. I made an appointment with a counselor. For a little while, I tried to act as if nothing was wrong, that I was just tired and feeling burned out. That's normal, right? Sharon wasn't fooled. The most incredible thing she told me was, "It's okay, Andrea; God says you don't have to try so hard." How badly I needed to hear that. I was just so tired.

Sharon gently, lovingly challenged me to confront the issues that drove me to hyperactivity. She helped me see that I had used activity (and ultimately simple "noise") to avoid facing my insecurities and fear of failure.

Before I sought help, I avoided stopping long enough to hear my heart breaking. Whenever feelings of worthlessness cropped up, whenever I felt out of control or thought no one could love me if they knew what a sinner I was, I simply got busier, assuming that losing myself for the sake of important, eternal things would help me feel better, *be* better.

And the world seemed to expect me to live with this frenetic, never-ending energy. Other people did. Didn't everyone have a "packed" schedule, a "killer" week, an "insane" semester? People ran from place to place trying to accomplish all they could as fast as they could. I just wanted to keep up. Plus, if I was busy, I felt important. Having something to do meant I was someone. Being bored meant I was boring, and I was *not* going to be boring.

During my burnout, though, nothing seemed to matter. My excitement for ministry and relationships and even my passion for Christ just evaporated. At that time, the thought often crossed my mind, *If I do nothing, at least I can't do anything wrong.*

Thank God He pulled me out when He did. Both the hyperspeed and wasted lifestyles wore on my soul. They not only impacted my schedule but also decimated my life in God. I couldn't really enjoy Him when I was too busy, though I stuck to my quiet time regime. And I couldn't even think about true prayer or meditation when life seemed overwhelming, pointless, and unfulfilling.

I learned, however, and continue to learn (because I am certainly not there yet) that in true quiet and stillness God speaks. Not in the silent, exhausted sense of nothingness I felt at twenty, but in the full, rich, alive serenity of His presence.

My present life and schedule demand much of me. I work with students. It would be easy to get sucked into their problems and their "I have to talk to you right now" timelines. There are times I'm tempted to throw up my hands and say, "Whatever; none of this really matters anyway." But God consistently woos me away with Him to be refreshed and stilled, to find sacred space whether I feel the pull of apathy and laziness or the harried anxiety of busyness.

Assessing the Disconnect

Do you ever find yourself hoping that people will cancel their appointments with you, simply so you'll have time to rest? Do you wish you had more time, or do you wish you could accomplish more and therefore need more time? Do you long for life beyond the delirious exertion of your energy?

Perhaps you've gotten into a habit of wasting time. Now you feel little motivation to do anything but be entertained. You watch soap operas and sitcoms, play video games, and paint your toenails every few days. Do you ever say, "There'll be time for everything else later"? Maybe you've thought to yourself, *Nothing really matters that much anyway, so why try?*

I have to confess right off: I am *sadly* ill equipped to write this chapter. I can write it only as another woman who *knows*, who feels the tension between frenetic scheduling and deep apathy.

We are often pulled, disconnected, not really certain of what's important and why. I once believed that if I did or achieved something, I was *someone*. I also assumed that if something was "godly," I should do it. Plus, the busier I was, the more I got done and the more important I became — right?

At other times I've invested way more time in trivial things than I care to admit. I didn't want to exert the energy to do anything but be amused. I've said "later" or "whatever" to things that actually would have given me the pleasure I sought had I only given them a chance.

I've lived out of many different lies about my time and energy. Have you? Are you ready to look at some of the most common misconceptions about how we use time?

Are These Lies Keeping You Frantic?

Because this chapter deals with both overactivity and underactivity, I've split the lies-versus-truth section in two. We'll start by confronting some toxic beliefs about busyness. While you read, keep in mind the truth we discovered in chapter 1: We do not increase our value by accomplishing many things, even important things. We are not worth the sum of our activities, even the most noble of our pursuits. God does not love us more because we do much, even if we do it "for Him." We are worth much because God says we are worth much.

This truth frees us from the bondage of having to perform, to be great, to be charming, to be what we think we need to be in order to get love and feel acceptable. And ironically, it frees us to do great things. When activity does not define you, when your focus shifts from proving your worth to doing what *really* matters at that moment, you discover God gives you the time, the power, and the energy to do it.

Lie 1: *Busyness is next to godliness.*

This insidious deception creeps into many minds and hearts: *If you're busy with godly things, you will be godly.* Sometimes my mind, the world, or the Enemy also whispers, *If you're busy with important, godly things, you will be valuable to other people* and *to God.*

When we do slow down for a moment, many of us have to choke back guilty thoughts: *You are so selfish. Don't you know that your neighbor just had a baby? You should take her a meal tonight.* Or *What a waste of a day you had. You neglected your family* [you didn't return an "urgent" phone call], *avoided your community responsibilities* [you forgot to vote], *and failed miserably to please your boss* [you were reprimanded for something at work]. *You didn't even have a quiet time. You are a waste.*

We easily believe this common assumption: Life is short, so work hard, play hard, live hard (and, for some, pray hard). But does striving not to waste a second make anyone happy? Fulfilled? Holier?

And who determines what a waste of time is, anyway?

Truth 1: *I find God when I live in and enjoy the present.*

As Andrea's story illustrates, even busying oneself with godly activities does not lead to personal fulfillment or intimacy with the Lord. In fact, overextension is one of the greatest enemies of God's work. Christ calls us to love, and one simply cannot love genuinely and deeply while running from place to place and person to person. Living in a world of feverishly strained overactivity does not encourage personal holiness either. As Christians, we are called to a sweeter life, a life calm enough to enjoy the "now."

I believe finding the schedule we crave begins with considering truths such as these:

This is what the Lord God, the Holy One of Israel, says:
"If you come back to me and trust me, you will be saved.
If you will be calm and trust me, you will be strong."
(Isaiah 30:15, NCV)

"Cease striving and know that I am God." (Psalm 46:10, NASB)

Do you long for rest? Do you want the strength of a quieter, calmer life? Do you yearn to cease striving so that you might know He is God?

Being fully "with God" is often quite challenging for me. When I rush from activity to activity (even if they are "godly" pursuits), I lose the joy of His presence in the anticipation of "what's next." I lose the beauty of the past, for no time is allotted to memory and reflection. And I lose the future moment to whatever is just beyond that. I live in constant limbo, and I miss the God who chooses to be found in the "now."

Hyperactive haste is not the same as godliness. The Word of God calls us to be still, to cease striving, and to find strength and rest in Him, whether that's in devotional reading, a quiet walk, prayer and praise, having a spa day, reading a book, or listening to music.

LIE 2: *I can do all things (or at least the really important ones).*

When I first became a Christian, my favorite verse was Philippians 4:13: "I can do all things through Christ who strengthens me" (NKJV). I interpreted this verse to mean, "God will give me the strength to do everything." I also subconsciously added this little tag: "*if* I need His strength." Because I could do a lot of things on my own, I sometimes lived as if I were saying, "Thank You, Lord, but I'll reserve Your strength for the times I really need it."

How many of you agree with this declaration of George MacDonald's: "When we wake and are weary, we say, 'Where is God?' And when we are strong and active and powerful, then we are ready to feel, 'Well, we can do without God today.'"[1] Personally, I have found that I can never do without God. I wish I could say I no longer try to live without Him, but I still do; I wish I could say I don't want to do without Him, but I still sometimes want to run my own show.

At times I manage my time well, giving myself and others the impression that I can handle things and live to do only *really* important things. But in reality, I often simply run back and forth between the catastrophic and the critical, forgetting who actually sustains me and knows what's most significant. I could die trying to do one more thing.

TRUTH 2: *I can do what God wants me to do . . .*

. . . which, by the way, isn't everything.

John 15:5 teaches that we can do nothing apart from Christ. I really had a hard time with this at first. Come on, nothing? Surely I can do the dishes and the cooking and the taxes (okay, maybe not the taxes) without God. "Nothing" seemed like a pretty big exaggeration to me. But consider this truth, found in Job 12:10:

> *In his hand is the life of every creature*
> *and the breath of all mankind.*

And these words from Psalm 3:5: "I wake again, because the LORD sustains me." It would be rather difficult to vacuum without life, breath, or even the simplest gift like waking up to a new day.

Okay, maybe this "I can do nothing" statement has something to it. While writing this chapter, I felt tempted to insert the word *meaningful* in front of *apart*. I can do nothing *meaningful* apart from God. That sounds better to my "I want to be important" mind. But the reality is, I can truly do *nothing* (no qualifiers) apart from Him. No one can. He sustains every life and breath. The Lord of all things has the right to determine my schedule and my priorities. And He'll give me the strength to do what matters to Him.

Do you know the story of Mary and Martha found in Luke 10:38-42? Basically, Martha is busting her buns trying to play "perfect hostess" for Jesus, while her sister sits at Christ's feet and listens. Martha, peeved like I would probably be, asks Jesus why He doesn't make her sister help. He replies, "Only one thing is important. Mary has chosen the better thing, and it will never be taken away from her" (verse 42, NCV).

"Really?" I want to ask. "You want me to sit at Your feet and listen and not do something for You—right now?" To me, listening to God always seemed risky because I was *sure* I wasn't doing enough or being good enough to please Him. I couldn't imagine Him saying, "Come, be with Me. I want to tell you the most wonderful thing."

Now I know the joy of sitting at Jesus' feet. I have been before His throne in prayer, in singing praises, in reading and writing. And I have also worshipped Him in physical, daily things such as running, mopping, kissing my children, and eating. In His presence I've found the greatest of pleasures (see Psalm 16:11).

One thing is most important; only one thing brings true fulfillment, full and lasting joy. Being in the present stillness with God—whether at church, work, or the park—is the only genuinely important thing. When we're near Jesus, we can find the schedule we crave.

Everything else can wait, perhaps should wait, until we hear from Christ Himself, "Go. Do this in My joy and peace." I wonder how different our schedules might look if we listened more and trusted that He will order our days well (see Psalm 90:12).

When You Say, "Whatever"

We've looked at what happens when we overcommit and fail to refresh. What happens when we couldn't care less? What happens when we're lethargic, sick of everything, unmotivated, and spiritually numb? And, as is often the case for me, what happens when "I'll do everything" dissolves into "I'll do nothing"?

We just learned that we don't have to do everything for God, but should we do nothing instead? By no means! Both overactivity and underactivity can be sins. It requires keen discernment and reliance on the Lord's Spirit to find the balance between "I'm going to conquer the world" and "Everything can wait (at least until this important program on the feeding habits of wallabies is over)."

When we find ourselves spiraling into indifference (and sometimes even boredom), we've probably been poisoned by one or both of the following toxic beliefs.

LIE 3: *My school, ministry, relationships, housework, _____ [fill in the blank] doesn't really matter that much.*

When I feel apathetic, I use phrases such as, "I don't care." "Whatever." "It doesn't matter." And at moments like these, I've settled for mere existence, forsaking true life.

The Bible has a word for this kind of attitude: *sloth*. What an ugly, awful word; I really wish I didn't have to use it, since I've already admitted this very attitude plagues me. Nonetheless, I looked up the synonyms for *sloth* and found these: *idleness, inactivity, laziness, apathy, indolence, lifelessness*. Hmmm . . . sounds like some of my recent bored, watching trashy TV, and/or overeating days. Is this the abundant life Christ died to give me?

Many times when we say, "It doesn't matter that much," what we really mean is, "It's too hard right now; I don't want to." Sloth tells us the lie that if something is difficult, we should find a way out of it (we reason that it's not *that* big of a deal). Sloth also tells us the lie that if we're doing nothing, we can't be doing anything wrong.

I have been guilty of sloth. I have majored in trivialities, neglecting the important for the easy. There have been mornings I just didn't want to be with Jesus, but I would have jumped out of bed to spend time with a friend or even exercise to maintain my figure. At other points, I couldn't have cared less about reading the Bible but would spend hours poring over magazines, coveting the things or looks others had.

We either choose sloth, or we choose to develop a vibrant life — the abundant life of the Spirit. And we make this decision day by day, even minute by minute. Ultimately, we *choose* to say either, "Here I am, Lord" or, "It doesn't really matter." And whatever decision we make changes us, even in the minutest way.

Truth 3: *My choices matter.*

We live in a society riddled with choices. For instance, I have a serious problem with those "just try to find a good doctor (and by the way, the one you want isn't in your network)" books that insurance companies provide. Don't even get me started.

When we moved to Colorado, I hadn't had a chance to get a recommendation from someone, so I attempted to pick the "right" doctor out of hundreds of options. I chose a general practitioner who also was an ob-gyn and who I was sure was a woman. I ended up with a man who had one of those confusing androgynous names and a little yippy dog that ran around the office during my pap smear. It was horrible! That choice clearly made a difference in my health-care experience. But what about the hundreds of other choices we are asked to make every day: pink or blue sticks on our Q-tips? Extra strength or maximum strength? Do they matter?

Barry Schwartz, author of *The Paradox of Choice*, says, "When people have no choice, life is almost unbearable. . . . But as the number of choices keeps growing, negative aspects of having a multitude of options begin to appear. . . . The negatives escalate until we become overloaded. At this point, choice no longer liberates, but debilitates. It might even be said to tyrannize."[2]

Amid the overwhelming number of decisions we must make, we can lose the truth that many of our choices really *do* matter. Lauren Winner articulates this brilliantly: "The choices we make every day — where we shop, what we do with our bodies, how we pass our time — form us.

They shape the type of Christians we become. . . . [Each choice] creates certain expectations in us, teaches us certain lessons."[3]

Living a passive life may bring temporary pleasure (and avoid some sin). But as Joyce Meyer so aptly notes,

> *There are aggressive sins, or sins of commission, and there are passive sins, which are sins of omission. In other words, there are wrong things that we do, and there are right things that we don't do. For example, a relationship can be destroyed by speaking thoughtless words, but it can also be destroyed by the omission of kind words of appreciation that should have been spoken but never were.*[4]

Scripture teaches that how we choose to live matters. Ephesians 5:15-16 warns and instructs us: "Be very careful, then, how you live — not as unwise but as wise, making the most of every opportunity." The phrase "making the most of every opportunity" does not mean swinging to the extreme of perpetual motion but rather recognizing that what you do and choose impacts how you live. Sloth majors in trivialities. Godly women want to know which decisions are important, and they humbly, prayerfully ask the Spirit to help them choose wisely.

With God's help, we can make wise choices in how we spend our time. In Psalm 119:37, David prays, "Turn my eyes away from worthless things." We can ask the Spirit to turn our eyes and our lives away from what is valueless. And we can choose to engage in activities that build us up and encourage us in faith, hope, and love (even if for me that sometimes means watching a favorite show or movie with Jeramy because it grows our love by just having fun together).

When sucked down by underactivity, I find it difficult to hope. Fearing that nothing will change, I sometimes refuse even to try to make a wise choice. "It doesn't matter anyway," I reason. "No matter what, it's all a waste."

What a tragic, heartbreaking deception.

It *does* matter. What I choose does matter, and what you choose matters, too.

LIE 4: *I'll have time for that later, or, I don't have time for that right now.*

Believing either of these two similar lies always leads to neglect. How we choose to spend our time reflects our priorities. When unmotivated and apathetic, I neglect my call as a woman of God. I neglect to care for my body and mind. I neglect loving others in favor of finding pleasure or attention for myself.

How often I've believed the terrible lie that I don't have time to spend with God or do His work. How often I've thought, *There will be plenty of opportunities when I feel "more into it" or "more excited about it."* Basically, what I'm doing is disobeying God.

Selective or delayed obedience allows us to become comfortable with corrupt thoughts and patterns as long as they aren't what we consider "big" sins. We make excuses for the "little" things we do or, maybe more often, neglect to do.

Have you ever apologized to someone (or given an "almost true" excuse) for arriving late, all the while knowing that you *decided* to show up a few minutes after you were supposed to? Maybe you waited so you could walk to the parking lot with your cute colleague. Is your selfish behavior a "little" sin? What about your "I'll do with my time what I want" attitude?

Can you think of a time you conveniently "forgot" to congratulate a friend on her recent success purely out of envy and spite? Did you make an excuse like this: *I'm sure she had enough people excited for her*? Have you ever neglected to return someone's phone call because you knew she was hurting and might need you? Did you assure yourself that you were far too busy and stressed out yourself? Maybe you thought, *I couldn't be a help to her anyway.*

D. L. Moody once preached, "If the devil can only get us off into some cradle of excuses and rock us off to sleep, that is all he wants."[5] And if we can convince ourselves or let others tempt us into believing that we have all the time in the world, Satan doesn't even have to bother tucking us into our snug, slothful beds.

We become accustomed to our schedules and don't want to be interrupted by the adventures of God. Sean Dunn, author of *Bored with God*, explains that "apathy dulls the spiritual senses and whispers lies of security to those who are infected. It is the door through which sin enters and faith leaves."[6]

Procrastinating, or majoring in the minors, can cause apathy or come as a result of preexisting indifference. The same is true of failure. When women become consumed by their past mistakes, they often figure, *If I can't live without messing up, I might as well stop trying*. On the flip side, they may not care very much to begin with, end up failing, and thus reinforce their "whatever" mentality.

Many women feel apathetic about their spiritual life for the same reasons. They may neglect their relationships with God or find them unfulfilling and resign themselves to a "tried it; it didn't work for me" attitude toward faith. Other women give up with thoughts like these: *I've worked really hard to please God, but I just keep flubbing up. The Christian life is too hard; why should I keep trying? I'm just going to blow it again.* In the first instance, apathetic neglect leads to greater indifference. In the second case, a failed attempt results in an apathetic spiral.

Failure, even perceived failure, often robs us of our ability to trust in ourselves and sometimes steals our desire to trust in God. This reinforces negative self-talk and makes us less and less able to hear what God says about us. Failure causes many of us to question our abilities and future. For some, it even dashes the hope that anything can change.

Has your walk with God ever been defined by an apathetic neglectfulness? When I embrace an "I don't have time for this right now" attitude, my life and my heart breaks down. God becomes a familiar pastime rather than a trusted friend and counselor. My faith becomes a religious hobby rather than a consuming passion.

TRUTH 4: *I can make time for God and what He wants me to do.*
Everyone makes time for the things he or she considers important, essential, or enjoyable. I make time for what I feel like I absolutely have to do or for what brings me pleasure. Why don't I focus more on the One who brings me lasting pleasure? This comment from Sean Dunn floored me: "When people become bored with God they seek excitement in other forms. . . . [They may] lack the desire to pursue spiritual things, but [they] never lack the craving to be entertained because it takes so little effort and discipline."[7] Many times after a hard day, I have thought, *I just want to escape; I just want to veg by watching TV or an old movie. I just want to be entertained so I don't have to think anymore.*

It's tragically ironic that we allow ourselves to become bored with God, for it is apathetic Christianity that creates the most joyless living imaginable. We cannot take true pleasure in our efforts or our leisure when disconnected from Joy Himself. We do not have the strength or courage to try new things when neglecting our walk with Christ. And we cannot find peace with ourselves, whether succeeding or failing at any given moment, if we have forsaken our first love. Joy, valor, and peace grow only as fruits of our intimacy with the Holy Spirit.

In Christ, and because of Him, I can do the things that matter. I can try and often succeed at things I may previously have avoided because I feared failure. And in Him, indifference and tedium can be replaced by a zest for and delight in life. Psalm 34:8 exclaims, "Taste and see that the LORD is good." Yahweh gives us drink from His "river of delights" (Psalm 36:8). He fills us with joy in His presence, with *eternal pleasures* at His right hand (see Psalm 16:11).

I can make time for this kind of God. I *want* to make time for this God, *my* God. Amen? He craves your presence, your intimacy, your love. He wants you to succeed and enjoy life (despite what many tragically joyless Christians might tempt you to believe).

Making time for God and what He calls us to do doesn't result in boredom, frustration, failure, or a dull life. First Timothy 6:17 encourages us, "Put [your] hope in God, who richly provides us with everything for our enjoyment." How amazingly, unbelievably wonderful is that?

When you surrender your time and energy to God and to the things He wants you to do and be, you discover that "obedience ... brings exquisite thrill."[8] I'd venture a guess that you'd be interested in something described as "exquisite thrill." I'd also venture a guess that you and I would be less afraid of failing if we focused on "being confident of this, that he who began a good work in you *will* carry it on to completion until the day of Christ Jesus" (Philippians 1:6, emphasis added). What an incredible thought: We can be confident in Him. All the events of our lives — whether we perceive them as victories or failures — *will* climax in a glorious success because He has planned it that way.

It's essential to note that just because you're a Christian doesn't mean you'll live without tasting failure. I fail — every day! But failure to succeed at one thing is only part of the story. The greater truth is that God is accomplishing His work in and through you. His plans will not fail.

He began a good work in you. And He will carry it on to completion. It doesn't depend on how well you do. Even if you make a terrible mistake or commit a heinous sin, His plans will never fail. If we live in that truth, releasing our indifference and embracing the One who calls us to do only that which He gives us the strength to accomplish, we will be willing to risk all that we are for love of Him. And *that* is adventurous living. May His joy renew us, and may we each find our spiritual lethargy drowned in a sea of consuming passion for and pleasure in Him.

What Can I Do?

- **Offer up your time to its rightful owner.** In his article "Time to Give Up," David W. Henderson retells the interaction between Jesus and the rich young ruler, found in Mark 10:17-31. He replaces the wealthy youth with an overextended young man whose schedule reveals that which he truly holds dear. He has time for moneymaking and self-promoting but little time for that which is truly important. Henderson paraphrases Mark 10:21 with these words: "'One thing you lack,' Jesus said. 'Go, clear your schedule of all your self-important activity. Then come and give all of your time to Me. Let Me order your days. Fill your life with what really matters. Follow Me.'"⁹ What really matters? Following Him. There is nothing else. Henderson claims that whether we are procrastinators or frenetically energized "doers," life is not about learning better time management but about learning to *let God manage our time.* As we acknowledge that our time does not belong to us, we may be less inclined to demand our "right" to do nothing or fulfill our "obligation" to do everything.

For the Overextended

- **Recognize your limits.** There are some people who can handle more activities than others. I am an energetic, highly focused, passionate person most of the time. But I have been forced to recognize that I have limits — physical, emotional, and even spiritual constraints. I have to be in touch with my limits and sensitive to cues that I'm headed for overload. And I can't always do it on my own. I need to believe and live out God's truth: Only one thing is important. But I also need people to tell me, "Jerusha, you've got to slow down." God often uses my husband, friends, and family to remind me that, try as I may, I will never be Wonder Woman (but, seriously, she did have the coolest outfit). All of us hyperactives need to realize that we cannot keep giving our hearts and taxing our bodies. Without rest we *will* break down.

- **Build margin into your schedule.** In other words, mentally discipline yourself to avoid calendar congestion. Some of us consistently book things one after another, leaving no space for the unexpected phone call or extra five minutes to offer a much-needed prayer. Dr. Richard Swenson defines margin so well: "Margin is the space between our load and our limits . . . the gap between rest and exhaustion. Margin is the opposite of overload."[10] We just can't do it all. Try with me, each day, to create margin. Do one less thing than you planned to do. Take the extra five minutes to enjoy something you may not have done if you were crunched for time. Start to find that gap between rest and exhaustion. Maybe if one by one we begin practicing margin, other women won't feel so pressured to keep up with the hyperactive lifestyle of others. I'm willing to go for it. Are you?

For the Unmotivated

- **Try doing something for a minute longer.** In one *Peanuts* cartoon, Charlie Brown confessed, "I used to try to take each day as it came, but my philosophy has changed. I'm down to half a day at a time."[11] I can relate. But unlike Charlie Brown, I can't even take half a day at a time; I admire his ability! I have to take one minute at a time. My amazing godmother and friend, Stephanie Edwards, once told me, "When I feel apathetic and unmotivated, I just try to do something for one minute longer than I would have (or maybe want to). I also try *not* to do something I'm tempted to do for one minute." What great wisdom and encouragement I've found in that! Sometimes I can do something I don't want to do longer than one minute more, just because I started with a small goal. And when I'm tempted, I often find that one minute of refusal to give in is all it takes to quell my craving. But no matter what the results, one more minute of obedience is pleasing to God.

- **Ask God to give you joy.** I love Nehemiah 8:10. It reads, "The joy of the LORD is your strength." You cannot manufacture motivation or desire. You can force yourself to do something, but without your heart's engagement, the activity will most likely be unfulfilling and may feel meaningless and empty. You gain strength through the joy that is found only in the Lord. He alone can give you the energy, focus, and *delight* you need to persevere and do what is important. Ask and you will receive. Seek His joy and you will find it. You will also discover strength for the task ahead.

⁓

You have taught us that in returning and rest we will be saved, in quietness and confidence we will be strengthened. By the power of Your Spirit, lift us to Your Presence, where we may be still and know that You are God. Amen.[12]

On That Thought . . .

1. Which tempts you more: overactivity or underactivity? Why do you think that is? Ask God to reveal to you some of the reasons why. Spend a few moments in silent reflection. If you're studying with others, share with the group and ask them to pray for you. If you're journaling, read your words to a trusted friend or mentor and ask for specific intercession.

2. Do you find it more difficult to say no or yes to things? Why? How would you define the term *balance*? What would your life look like if you were more balanced?

3. Interact with these thoughts based on your life experience, both past and present:

> *Why has your life suddenly lost its zeal? Are your hands hanging limply at your sides? Is that your voice sighing in the night and whispering furtively in the darkness, "I don't care anymore?" But you do care! You do have deep and intense interests. You have merely lost hope. Hope deferred makes the heart sick. . . . Desire fulfilled is . . . life. I am your life. In Me you will find hope for the future and joy for the present.*[13]

> *Becoming busy . . . can make My servants too busy for Me. [Even] serving Me can bring about pressures you cannot handle in your human strength and talent. . . . But I am here, waiting for your call. I wait for all of your heart [and your time], not just part of it. Oh lukewarm, storm-tossed, cast-down. We rejoice over you. Have you forgotten how to dance to the heartbeat of heaven? . . . Come back to Me, come running back! I will give you time for what you truly need.*[14]

4. Reflect on a period in your life when you felt particularly overextended. What emotions and physical sensations did you experience? Did you thrive off or feel weighed down by your overactivity? What did your busyness do to your relationships with others? Your relationship with God? If you had the chance to advise that former you, what would you say? What would Christ say to you?

5. Look back to a time in your life when you felt apathetic. Again, what emotions and physical sensations did you experience? What

did your lethargy do to your relationships with others? Your relationship with God? If you had the chance to advise that former you, what would you say? What would Christ say to you?

Every Thought Captive

A Benediction

Although it is important and even indispensable for our spiritual lives to set apart time for God and God alone, our prayer can only become unceasing communion when all our thoughts — beautiful or ugly, high or low, proud or shameful, sorrowful or joyful — can be thought in the presence of the One who dwells in us and surrounds us. By trying to do this, our unceasing thinking is converted into unceasing prayer moving us from a self-centered monologue to a God-centered dialogue. To do this we want to try to convert our thoughts into conversation. The main question, therefore, is not so much what we think, but to whom we present our thoughts . . . to think and live in the presence of Love.

HENRY NOUWEN

In chapter 1, I proposed we explore the mystery of taking every thought captive to Christ. I hope that as you've read, the Holy Spirit has illuminated that phrase. Through my own journey of researching and writing this book, praying and agonizing, God gave me a few ideas about thinking with a captivated mind. I'd love to share them with you as a benediction.

A recurrent theme in my quiet times, spiritual reading, and conversations has been the idea of Christ as my "first love." This concept reveals two important facets of loving God: one, we should love nothing and no one above God; and two, we experience His love and reflect it back as if falling in love with Him for the first time over and over again.

When I fell for Jeramy almost a decade ago, I thought about him all the time. I wrote him a love poem while substitute teaching. When he held my hand, I sometimes couldn't focus on anything else. I thought about what we would do and talk about, how I could communicate my affection for him. My thoughts were often *consumed* with him. I was captivated by the thrill of falling in love for the first time.

Thoughts of him also expelled many other considerations from my mind. I simply didn't have room for less important things. Likewise, when we feel consumed with love for God, we have little room or tolerance for toxic beliefs. Christ utterly captivates our minds.

The word *captivate* means "influence or dominate... with an irresistible appeal."[1] We are either captives to Truth or to the father of lies. As we find God more irresistibly appealing than anything else, our minds are influenced and dominated by Him. And we've seen clearly that every thought shapes our lives. Because He *is* Love and Grace, Hope and Peace, our thoughts reflect these beautiful attributes.

The psalmist cries out,

> *I want to drink God,*
> > *deep draughts of God.*
> *I'm thirsty for God-alive.*
> *I wonder, "Will I ever make it —*
> > *arrive and drink in God's presence?" (42:1-2,* MSG)

> *When can I go and meet with God? (42:2)*

A first-love, captivated mind wonders, *When can I steal away to meet with God? How can I experience more of Him?*

I used to rearrange my schedule — turn my day upside down — to meet with Jeramy. I wanted to drink deeply from his love. I couldn't imagine ever getting enough of him. God wants this same thinking to define my relationship with Him.

Somewhat ironically, the only way I learned to hunger and thirst for God was to start spending time with Him. As I tasted and saw that the Lord was good (see Psalm 34:8), I longed to imbibe more deeply of Him, the fountain of Life.

As you drink from His "river of delights" (Psalm 36:8), you will find less and less satisfaction in drinking the paltry, unsatisfying dregs of sinful thoughts. When your mind becomes captivated, there will be less room for faulty thinking. This is the first image the Lord gave me of a captivated mind — a mind intoxicated by "first love."

After carefully considering the words *captivity* and *captive*, God revealed to me another aspect of taking every thought captive. Being in captivity "makes departure or inattention difficult."[2] A captive has been forcefully brought under the control of an authority greater than her own. She is "owned or controlled by another concern and operated for its needs."[3]

I used to imagine myself taking thoughts prisoner and leading them to Christ. This mental picture still helps me at times. But this image relied a great deal on me. I may have known I could take thoughts captive only by God's strength, but I often lived as if it really depended on me to bring flawed notions to His throne.

Now I picture Jesus as my mind's captor, with all my thoughts in willing captivity to Him. In captivity to my Lord, "departure or inattention is difficult." As a captive of Christ's, I am "owned or controlled by another concern, an authority greater than my own." I am "operated for" His design — freedom through truth (see John 8:32).

When I'm captivated, a thought that does not align with the truth of God cannot easily steal my attention from the concern that owns and operates me. Though my mind may still make departures into uncaptivated thinking, leaving the captivity of Christ proves more and more unfulfilling. Only as His captive can I find lasting freedom from the bondage of toxic beliefs.

A final aspect of taking every thought captive centers around who Christ is. When Jesus proclaimed in John 14:6, "I am the way, the truth, and the life" (NLT), He gave us a standard against which we can judge the passing notions of our minds. He *is* the Truth. In Him there is no shadow of deception, no shade of flawed thinking. Because our God *is* Truth, He helps us evaluate whether each of our thoughts is a truth or a lie. As we continue to surrender our minds in captivity to Christ, we begin to take questionable thoughts immediately to Truth Himself.

To live with a captivated mind, we practice considering our thoughts before we live out of them. Though we sometimes seem to act before we think, we really can act only after we consider. We always think, even if not enough, before we do something.

Thank goodness there will be some thoughts we can deal with quickly. Some ideas will be obviously true; others are clearly lies. But a lot of the things we think on a regular basis are veiled deceptions. We either haven't pinpointed them as lies, or we have become so accustomed to thinking them that we cannot objectively evaluate their validity. These are the most deadly toxic beliefs. For instance, I became so used to my brain responding to stress or perceived failure with the thoughts *I feel ugly* or *I feel fat* that I didn't recognize that these phrases masked deeper deceptions that plagued my heart: *If I fail, I'll be rejected*; *If I can't control my life, it will fall apart*; *If people find out who I really am, they won't love me.*

Through the chapters you've read, have you been able to identify some "default" phrases in your mind? I've told you some of mine. Yours may be entirely different. And they may be so familiar that you haven't questioned them in a long time; maybe you've never asked if the words in your head were true or false.

I pray that through this book you've found hope and encouragement to begin the process of filtering and evaluating your thoughts against the standard of Truth. This process will be ongoing and will last as long as God is transforming your mind.

Jean Nicholas Grou describes sanctification, which includes the renewal of our minds, as the active way.[4] He says that, like Jacob, we must wrestle with the God who purifies and strengthens us (see Genesis 32:22-31). We must wrestle with our thoughts until God blesses us with a peaceful, holy, captivated mind. As we battle, He *will* — piecemeal and progressively — transform our minds. He is transforming your mind even now. And though I use the words *wrestle* and *battle*, the process of transformation is life giving and hopeful rather than what we often imagine it will be — draining, painful, and exhausting. When Jacob wrestled with the Lord, he did so to receive God's *blessing*. We can fight the good fight with anticipation, motivated by the blessings that will be ours: freedom, new life, and unbridled joy.

Lies still assault me. I assume they will until my mind is perfectly redeemed in glory. Sometimes I give in to the toxic beliefs. I fail. We will all fail. The Enemy of our souls, people in our lives, and our own flawed-until-we-reach-heaven minds may attempt to cripple us with self-accusation. The Enemy may remind you of the darkness of your past thoughts. But believe with me: We cannot judge our lives only by their darkest corners.

Great painters of the Renaissance, such as Caravaggio, employed a technique called chiaroscuro to contrast light and dark. The power of their paintings often came from the shadows, created by meticulous shading and sometimes piercing blackness. Yet every stroke of darkness allowed the light to shine more brilliantly. The canvas of your life will be marked by both the shadows of humanity and the light of redemption. Step back. Look at the whole picture. See how the contrast of darkness and light reveals the radiance and splendor of the one pure Light.

A captivated mind won't be yours overnight. But God's design for your mind *will* be fulfilled. There may be times when you despair; I have known deep despair. At other times, perhaps you'll try — as I have often done — to run ahead of Grace, attempting to fix your own problems and redeem your own mind. Sometimes you may, like me, refuse to let Him have your thoughts. But whether or not you can see it, even if you blew it yesterday, He *is* moving in you today.

When the prophet Habakkuk became discouraged because he didn't think God was acting quickly enough, the Lord responded, "These things I plan won't happen right away. Slowly, steadily, surely, the time approaches when the vision will be fulfilled. If it seems slow, do not despair, for these things will surely come to pass. Just be patient! They will not be overdue a single day!" (2:3, TLB).

What happened yesterday and what will happen tomorrow do not matter as much as what you choose *now*, in this very moment, where God meets you and promises to satisfy your most intimate desires. Never stop pursuing the life you crave, the life Christ died to give you.

While you chase the freedom and transformed mind that you long for, you will have some pain. But you will also have times of exhilarating joy, beautiful revelation, and greater peace than you have ever experienced. Times like these keep me going when the battle rages hot and furious. Times like these allow me to taste and see that the Lord is good (see Psalm 34:8), that He is doing something good in me.

Our Light and Hope declares, "I am holding you by your right hand — I, the LORD your God . . . am here to help you" (Isaiah 41:13, NLT). Imagine Jesus, the Almighty God, holding your hand. He is there, even when your thoughts seem overwhelming again. In Him you *will* find victory. In Him you *will* overcome. Even your darkness will reveal His Light more powerfully. Let Him take your mind captive.

I love these words, inspired by Emily Dickinson: "There is, in the end, the letting go." When it all boils down, I must let go of all my attempts to control life. There is no other way. I must surrender to be captivated by the One who steadies, upholds, and rejoices with me in victory. I must have *Life*. Amen.

Helps for the Journey

Anderson, Fil. *Running on Empty: Contemplative Spirituality for Overachievers*. Colorado Springs, CO: WaterBrook, 2004.

> *I devoured Anderson's book. His words are healing and true.*

Ashcroft, Mary Ellen. *Temptations Women Face: Honest Talk About Jealousy, Anger, Sex, Money, Food, Pride*. Downers Grove, IL: InterVarsity, 1991.

> *A look at the seven deadly sins from a feminine perspective. I especially like her treatment of greed.*

Buechner, Frederick. *Telling Secrets: A Memoir*. New York: HarperCollins, 1991.

> *In my opinion, few writers use words as brilliantly and evocatively as Buechner. Even fewer are as vulnerable with their pain as he is. The truths about despair and life that Buechner explores were tremendously helpful in processing my own depression.*

Geegh, Mary. *God Guides*. Holland, MI: Missionary Press, 1996.

> *I love this thin but powerful book. Geegh's statement, "When man listens, God speaks; When man obeys, God acts; When God acts, men change,"[1] transformed the way I looked at devotional time, listening, and obedience.*

Kadlecek, Jo. *Fear: A Spiritual Navigation.* Colorado Springs, CO: Shaw Books, 2001.

> *This book is both riveting and beautifully written. Kadlecek's insights are woven through story and memory.*

Kelley, Thomas R. *A Testament of Devotion.* New York: HarperSanFrancisco, 1992. First published 1941.

> *A spiritual classic — and for good reason. Kelley poignantly and transparently describes his battle to sustain an inner turning to God amid the everyday concerns of life.*

Manning, Brennan. *Abba's Child: The Cry of the Heart for Intimate Belonging.* Colorado Springs, CO: NavPress, 2002.

> *Because both deep suffering and profound spiritual experiences have marked Manning's life, his book is authentic and healing.*

McGee, Robert S. *The Search for Significance: Seeing Your True Worth Through God's Eyes.* Houston: Rapha Publishing, 1990.

> *I would buy a copy for every woman I know if I could.*

Michael, Chester P., and Marie C. Norrisey. *Prayer and Temperament: Different Prayer Forms for Different Personality Types.* Charlottesville, VA: Open Door Inc., 1991.

> *If you long to pray more or to experience a deeper level of communion with God, this book will inspire and instruct you.*

Pintus, Lorraine, and Linda Dillow. *Gift-Wrapped by God: Secret Answers to the Question "Why Wait?"* Colorado Springs, CO: WaterBrook, 2003.

——— *Intimate Issues: 21 Questions Women Ask About Sex.* Colorado Springs, Co: WaterBrook, 1999.

These books are uplifting and meditative, yet practical and honest—must-reads. Note: Gift-Wrapped is geared for younger women (mostly single), so if you're older and/or married, you may want to read Intimate Issues.

Rhodes, Constance. *Life Inside the "Thin" Cage: A Personal Look into the Hidden World of the Chronic Dieter.* Colorado Springs, CO: Shaw Books, 2003.

This book is tremendously insightful and intimately written; I highly recommend Life Inside for all women. Rhodes also hosts a website, www.findingbalance.com, which serves women eager to break free from the oppression of unhealthy body image.

Smedes, Lewis B. *The Art of Forgiving: When You Need to Forgive and Don't Know How.* New York: Ballantine Books, 1996.

——— *Forgive and Forget: Healing the Hurts We Don't Deserve.* New York: HarperSanFrancisco, 1997.

I recommend these books together because I would not want anyone to miss the insights in either of them. Smedes humbly, evocatively asks and answers many of the deepest questions about forgiveness.

Winner, Lauren F. *Real Sex: The Naked Truth About Chastity.* Grand Rapids, MI: Brazos Press, 2005.

Winner's biblical, smart, funny, brass-tacks, tell-it-like-it-is book on chastity will reorder your thinking about sex.

Notes

CHAPTER 1: ON MY MIND

1 Joyce Meyer, *Battlefield of the Mind: Winning the Battle in Your Mind* (New York: Warner Faith, 2002), 69.

2 Elizabeth George, *Loving God with All Your Mind* (Eugene, OR: Harvest House, 1994), 15.

3 Chester P. Michael and Marie C. Norrisey, *Prayer and Temperament: Different Prayer Forms for Different Personality Types* (Charlottesville, VA: Open Door Inc., 1991), 8.

4 See verses such as 1 John 4:16: "God is love" (NLT); John 14:6: "I am the way, the truth, and the life" (NLT); and Psalm 71:5: "For you have been my hope, O Sovereign LORD."

5 Thomas R. Kelly, *A Testament of Devotion* (1941; repr., New York: HarperSanFrancisco, 1992), 13.

6 "Before Worship," prayer 64 in *The Book of Common Prayer* (1789; repr., New York: Oxford University Press, 1990), 833.

7 Frederick Buechner, "Silence of the Holy Place" in *Listening to Your Life* (New York: HarperSanFrancisco, 1992), 332.

CHAPTER 2: GOOD ENOUGH

1 This phrase comes from Robert S. McGee's excellent book *The Search for Significance: Seeing Your True Worth Through God's Eyes* (Houston: Rapha Publishing, 1990).

2   Randy Rowland, *The Sins We Love: Embracing Brokenness, Hoping for Wholeness* (New York: Doubleday, 2000), 94.

3   Some of you may wonder how one can reconcile the conclusion to this parable with the vision of a lavishly loving God. As the story closes, Jesus relates that the master takes the one talent given to this servant, calls him "worthless," and commands that he be thrown "outside, into the darkness, where there will be weeping and gnashing of teeth" (Matthew 25:28-30). We must understand that in this parable, the third servant represents the unbelieving person. God has entrusted even those who do not confess and believe on the name of Jesus with talents and abilities. Those who are sealed with the Holy Spirit receive special, spiritual gifts (see Romans 12:6-8; 1 Corinthians 12:1-29). Consequently, they have more "talents" like the first and second servants. True children of God invest their lives (to some degree, depending on the maturity of their faith) in eternal purposes. Unbelievers do not use their talents for the glory of God (thus burying what God has given them) and will be judged according to their lack of faith in God. The third servant does not believe that the character of God is good, loving, and true. He does not believe in the living Lord. His condemnation is the natural outcome of His denial of the true Master. As a Christian, you are *not* the third servant. You can, however, be deceived and believe like him for any length of time. At different points in my life, I have "buried" my talents, not really believing that God was who He revealed Himself to be. I *acted* like the third servant, but thanks be to God, I did not become him. After I awoke to the truth of who I am and who He is, I began to fulfill my destiny as one of the faithful servants. Wherever you are, at this very moment, you can choose to believe that God is the God the first two servants believed Him to be or the harsh and demanding master the third servant envisioned Him to be. You choose. And remember, your choice will change you.

4 Madeleine L'Engle, *A Live Coal in the Sea* (San Francisco: HarperSanFrancisco, 1997).

5 Thomas Merton, *The Hidden Ground of Love: Letters of Religious Experience and Social Concerns* (New York: Farrar, Strauss, Giroux, 1985), 146, emphasis added.

6 John Eagan, *A Traveler Toward the Dawn: The Spiritual Journal of John Eagan, S. J.* (Chicago: Loyola University Press, 1990), 150–151.

7 Brennan Manning, *Abba's Child: The Cry of the Heart for Intimate Belonging* (Colorado Springs, CO: NavPress, 1994), 26.

8 David A. Seamands, *Healing for Damaged Emotions: Recovering from the Memories That Cause Our Pain* (Colorado Springs, CO: Chariot Victor, 1991), 86.

9 I want to clarify that surrendering to God does not mean inviting everyone who has wounded us back into our lives, close enough to injure us again. For more on this, please look at chapter 5, which contrasts bitterness and forgiveness.

10 Seamands, 15.

11 Anonymous.

CHAPTER 3: WORRIED

1 National Institute of Mental Health, "The Numbers Count: Mental Disorders in America," www.nimh.nih.gov/publicat/numbers.cfm (updated June 10, 2005).

2 The Association of Women's Health, Obstetric and Neonatal Nurses and Profile Pursuit Inc., "Finding Your Balance," *Every Woman: The Essential Guide for Healthy Living*, Winter 2004, 93–98.

3   *International Standard Bible Encyclopedia*, s.v. "Care: I. In the sense of Anxiety, Solicitude," accessed through Quick Verse 8.0 Deluxe.

4   *Webster's New Collegiate Dictionary* (Springfield, MA: G. & C. Merriam Webster Company, 1981), s.v. "Fear."

5   *Webster's New Collegiate Dictionary*, s.v. "Care."

6   It's highly significant to note that almost all of these instances encourage believers *not* to fear. The majority of those remaining command us to hold the Lord in reverential, loving fear.

7   Anna Sewell, *Black Beauty* (1877; repr., New York: Sterling Publishing Co., Inc., 2004), 108.

8   Gregory L. Jantz, PhD, *Hope, Help, and Healing for Eating Disorders: A New Approach to Treating Anorexia, Bulimia, and Overeating* (Colorado Springs, CO: Shaw Books, 2002), 27.

9   Jeremiah 31:17, NASB.

10 Edward W. Goodrick, John R. Kohlenberger III, and James A. Swanson, assoc. ed., *Zondervan NIV Exhaustive Concordance*, 2nd ed. (Grand Rapids, MI: Zondervan, 1999), s.v. "Sovereign."

11 W. E. Vine, *Vine's Expository Dictionary of New Testament Words* (McLean, VA: MacDonald Publishing Company, n.d.), 424, s.v. "Phobos."

12 *The Random House Unabridged Dictionary*, 2nd ed., s.v. "Worry."

13 Jo Kadlecek, *Fear: A Spiritual Navigation* (Colorado Springs, CO: Shaw Books, 2001), 4.

14 Phyllis Tickle, comp., *The Divine Hours: Prayers for Springtime* (New York: Doubleday, 2001), 124.

CHAPTER 4: ONE MORE THING

1 Mary Ellen Ashcroft, *Temptations Women Face: Honest Talk About Jealousy, Anger, Sex, Money, Food, Pride* (Downers Grove, IL: InterVarsity, 1991), 55.

2 Elisabeth Elliot, *Let Me Be a Woman* (Wheaton, IL: Tyndale, 1976), 42.

3 Adaptation of "For the Right Use of God's Gifts," prayer 38 in *The Book of Common Prayer*, (1789; repr., New York: Oxford University Press, 1990), 827.

CHAPTER 5: OFFENDED

1 Walter A. Elwell, ed., *Evangelical Dictionary of Theology* (Grand Rapids, MI: Baker, 1984), s.v. "Forgiveness"; *Theological Dictionary of the New Testament*, ed. Gerhard Kittel and Gerhard Friedrich, trans. Geoffrey W. Bromiley (Grand Rapids, MI: Eerdmans, 1985), 747.

2 Lewis B. Smedes, *The Art of Forgiving: When You Need to Forgive and Don't Know How* (New York: Ballantine Books, 1996), 59.

3 Frederick Buechner, "Forgiveness" in *Listening to Your Life* (New York: HarperSanFrancisco, 1992), 305.

4 Smedes, *The Art of Forgiving*, 90–91.

5 This phrase comes from a book by Lewis Smedes, somewhat ironically titled *Forgive and Forget: Healing the Hurts We Don't Deserve* (New York: HarperSanFrancisco, 1997).

6 David A. Seamands, *Healing for Damaged Emotions: Recovering from the Memories That Cause Our Pain* (Colorado Springs, CO: Chariot Victor, 1991), 134.

7 Frank E. Gæbelein, ed., *The Expositor's Bible Commentary* (Grand Rapids, MI: Zondervan, 1984), 405.

8 Smedes, *The Art of Forgiving*, 162.

9 Smedes, *Forgive and Forget*, 83.

10 *Random House Webster's Collegiate Dictionary*, 2nd ed., s.v. "Forgive."

11 Ellen Michaud, "Discover the Power of Forgiveness," *Prevention Magazine*, January 1999, 110–115.

12 Mary Geegh, *God Guides*, 12th ed. (1970; repr., Holland, MI: Missionary Press, 1996), 44.

CHAPTER 6: ACCEPTED

1 *Webster's New Collegiate Dictionary* (Springfield, MA: G. & C. Merriam Webster Company, 1981), s.v. "Loneliness," "Lonely," Lonesome."

2 *Webster's New Collegiate Dictionary*, s.v. "Affliction."

3 Jane Austen, *Emma* (1815; repr., New York: Barnes & Noble Classics, 2004), 19.

4 David A. Seamands, *Healing for Damaged Emotions: Recovering from the Memories That Cause Our Pain* (Colorado Springs, CO: Chariot Victor, 1991), 21.

5 Mary Ellen Ashcroft, *Temptations Women Face: Honest Talk About Jealousy, Anger, Sex, Money, Food, Pride* (Downers Grove, IL: InterVarsity, 1991), 117.

6 Ashcroft, 123.

7 The Westminster Assembly, *The Westminster Shorter Catechism*, 1647, first answer, accessed through Quick Verse 8.0 Deluxe.

8   *The Westminster Shorter Catechism.*

9   Jane Austen, *Persuasion* (1817; repr., New York: Norton, 1995), 155.

10 Lauren Winner, *Girl Meets God: A Memoir* (Colorado Springs, CO: Shaw Books, 2003), 85.

11 Attributed to Saint Francis of Assisi.

CHAPTER 7: ON FIRE

1   *Webster's New Collegiate Dictionary* (Springfield, MA: G. & C. Merriam Webster Company, 1981), s.v. "Lust."

2   Joshua Harris, *Not Even a Hint: Guarding Your Heart Against Lust* (Sisters, OR: Multnomah, 2003), 10.

3   Lauren F. Winner, *Real Sex: The Naked Truth About Chastity* (Grand Rapids, MI: Brazos Press, 2005), 15.

4   Linda Dillow and Lorraine Pintus, *Gift-Wrapped by God: Secret Answers to the Question "Why Wait?"* (Colorado Springs, CO: WaterBrook, 2002), 22–23.

5   Linda Dillow and Lorraine Pintus, *Intimate Issues: 21 Questions Christian Women Ask About Sex* (Colorado Springs, CO: WaterBrook, 1999), 10.

6   I paraphrase Willard only to pull his words into a concise definition of true sexual intimacy. I highly recommend you read *The Divine Conspiracy* not merely for its wisdom on this subject but also to explore Willard's amazing insights on the spiritual life as a whole.

7   Winner, 81.

8   Winner, 17–18.

9   Randy Rowland, *The Sins We Love: Embracing Brokenness, Hoping for Wholeness* (New York: Doubleday, 2000), 166.

10 After deliberation, reading on the subject, and interviews with women of different ages and personalities, I have come to the conclusion that masturbation is sin in some instances and not in others. I do not believe masturbation is universally right or wrong. For an excellent treatment on this subject, I refer you to Dr. Steve Gerali's book *The Struggle* (Colorado Springs, CO: NavPress, 2003).

11 Winner, 116–117.

12 Harris, 17.

13 John Piper, *Future Grace* (Sisters, OR: Multnomah, 1995), 336.

14 Marie Chapian, "In Times of Temptation" and "Too Busy" in *His Thoughts Toward Me* (Minneapolis: Bethany, 1987), 33–34, 126.

CHAPTER 8: SHAPED

1   This is Manning's paraphrase of Cardinal Wolsey's words.

2   Carolyn Costin, *The Eating Disorder Sourcebook: A Comprehensive Guide to the Causes, Treatments, and Prevention of Eating Disorders* (Los Angeles: Lowell House, 1999), 83.

3   C. M. Shisslak, M. Crago, and L. S. Estes, "The Spectrum of Eating Disturbances," *International Journal of Eating Disorders* 18, no. 3 (November 1995): 209.

4   Mary Pipher, *Hunger Pains* (Holbrook, MA: Adams Publishing, 1995), 12; National Eating Disorders Association, "General Eating Disorders Information," 2002, http://www.nationaleatingdisorders .org/p.asp?WebPage_ID=291.

5   National Institute of Mental Health, "Eating Disorders: Facts About Eating Disorders and the Search for Solutions," www.nimh.nih.gov/publicat/eatingdisorders.cfm (updated September 1, 2005).

6   Costin, 15.

7   Per a conversation between the author and a student who attended this university.

8   Dr. Alan Schwitzer, quoted in Constance Rhodes, *Life Inside the "Thin" Cage: A Personal Look into the Hidden World of the Chronic Dieter* (Colorado Springs, CO: Shaw Books, 2003), 22.

9   Sharon Hersh, quoted in Rhodes, 22.

10 Marya Hornbacher, *Wasted: A Memoir of Anorexia and Bulimia* (New York: Harper Perennial, 1998), 283.

11 Costin, 53.

12 Rhodes, 30.

13 Thanks to Antonina Ruth Bruno for sharing her thoughts about and experiences with these matters.

14 Rhodes, 49–50.

15 Mary Ellen Ashcroft, *Temptations Women Face: Honest Talk About Jealousy, Anger, Sex, Money, Food, Pride* (Downers Grove, IL: InterVarsity, 1991), 78.

16 Dr. Steven Bratman, quoted in ANRED: Anorexia Nervosa and Related Eating Disorders, Inc., "Less-well-known eating disorders and related problems," www.anred.com/defslesser.html (updated November 2004).

17 Rhodes, 45.

18 John and Stasi Eldredge, *Captivating: Unveiling the Mystery of a Woman's Soul* (Nashville: Nelson, 2005), 136.

19 Adaptation of "For the Victims of Addiction," prayer 831 in *The Book of Common Prayer* (1789; repr., New York: Oxford University Press, 1990), 831.

CHAPTER 9: OVERWHELMED

1 National Institute of Mental Health, "The Numbers Count: Mental Disorders in America," www.nimh.nih.gov/publicat/numbers.cfm (updated June 10, 2005).

2 National Institute of Mental Health, "Depression: What Every Woman Should Know," 2000, http://www.nimh.nih.gov/publicat/depwomenknows.cfm (updated September 2, 2005).

3 Jesse Dillinger, "Depression: The Basics" (Tape one of two lectures titled "Depression and the Christian," Jesse Dillinger Enterprises, San Diego, CA, 2004).

4 *Webster's New Collegiate Dictionary* (Springfield, MA: G. & C. Merriam Webster Company, 1981), s.v. "Depression."

5 Dillinger.

6 "For a Sick Person," in *The Book of Common Prayer* (1789; repr., New York: Oxford University Press, 1990), 458.

CHAPTER 10: IN TIME

1 George MacDonald, *Getting to Know Jesus* (New York: Ballantine Books, 1987), 31.

2 Barry Schwartz, quoted in "Time Lines," *Discipleship Journal*, January/February 2005, 57.

3 Lauren F. Winner, *Real Sex: The Naked Truth About Chastity* (Grand Rapids, MI: Brazos Press, 2005), 109.

4 Joyce Meyer, *Battlefield of the Mind: Winning the Battle in Your Mind* (New York: Warner Faith, 2002), 150.

5 D. L. Moody, quoted in Reverend J. Wilbur Chapman, D.D., "Three Characteristic Sermons," *The Life and Work of Dwight Lyman Moody* (originally published in 1900; accessed on http://www .biblebelievers.com/moody/22.html).

6 Sean Dunn, *Bored with God: How Parents, Youth Leaders, and Teachers Can Overcome Student Apathy* (Downers Grove, IL: InterVarsity, 2004), 14.

7 Dunn, 42.

8 Mary Geegh, *God Guides*, 12th ed. (1970; repr., Holland, MI: Missionary Press, 1996), 9.

9 David W. Henderson, "Time to Give Up," *Discipleship Journal*, January/February 2005, 46.

10 Richard A. Swenson, "I Know I'm Crunched for Time But . . .," *Discipleship Journal*, January/February 2005, 58.

11 Elizabeth George, *Loving God with All Your Mind* (Eugene, OR: Harvest House, 1994), 65.

12 Adaptation of "Prayer for Quiet Confidence," prayer 59 in *The Book of Common Prayer* (1789; repr., New York: Oxford University Press, 1990), 832.

13 Marie Chapian, "When Weariness Overtakes You" in *His Thoughts Toward Me* (Minneapolis: Bethany, 1987), 137.

14 Chapian, "Too Busy" in *His Thoughts Toward Me*, 126.

EVERY THOUGHT CAPTIVE: A BENEDICTION

1 *Webster's New Collegiate Dictionary* (Springfield, MA: G. & C. Merriam Webster Company, 1981), s.v. "Captivate."

2 *Webster's New Collegiate Dictionary*, s.v. "Captivity."

3 *Webster's New Collegiate Dictionary*, s.v. "Captive."

4 Jean Nicholas Grou, quoted in Thomas R. Kelly, *A Testament of Devotion* (1941; repr., New York: HarperSanFrancisco, 1992), 32.

APPENDIX: HELPS FOR THE JOURNEY

1 Mary Geegh, *God Guides*, 12th ed. (1970; repr., Holland, MI: Missionary Press, 1996), 7.

ABOUT THE AUTHOR

Jerusha Clark has partnered with her husband, Jeramy, to author four books and contribute a chapter to one other. She ministers to and with young women ages sixteen to thirty at Emmanuel Faith Community Church. Jerusha loves to teach others about the freedom found in confronting toxic lies and living out the truth. The mother of two toddlers and wife of a youth pastor, Clark leads a full and active life in Escondido, California.

DISCOVER GOD'S PLAN FOR YOUR LIFE.

Redefining Life: My Relationships
TH1NK
1-57683-888-9
There are no easy answers when it comes to relationships. But you can develop strong godly habits to prevent relationship drama before it begins. Learn how you can be a better friend, roommate, or girlfriend with this practical, advice-filled study.

Redefining Life: My Identity
TH1NK
1-57683-828-5
There is freedom in knowing who you are, and this discussion guide will help with the process. You'll not only discover what you were created for but also learn about the One who created you.

TH1NK

NAVPRESS®
BRINGING TRUTH TO LIFE
www.navpress.com